# THE MOLINEUX

# ENCYCLOPEDIA

Other titles available in this series

# THE MOLINEUX ENCYCLOPEDIA

## An A-Z of
### Wolverhampton Wanderers

*Dean Hayes*

MAINSTREAM
PUBLISHING

EDINBURGH AND LONDON

To Wolves fans everywhere!

First published in Great Britain in 1999 by
MAINSTREAM PUBLISHING COMPANY (EDINBURGH) LTD
7 Albany Street
Edinburgh EH1 3UG

ISBN 1 84018 142 7

The cover photographs have been kindly supplied by the *Wolverhampton Express
and Star*. Other photographs in the book have been supplied by the *Lancashire Evening
Post*, or are from the author's personal collection.

A catalogue record for this book is available from the British Library

Typeset in Janson Text
Printed and bound in Great Britian by The Cromwell Press Ltd

**ABANDONED MATCHES** A match may be called off by the referee whilst it is in progress, because conditions do not permit it to be completed. Generally speaking, far fewer matches are now abandoned because if there is some doubt about playing the full game, the match is more likely to be postponed. Wolves were involved in the shortest game on record when playing Stoke in a monstrous blizzard in 1894. Only 400 hardy souls braved the elements and they were mightily relieved when referee Mr Helme called off the proceedings after just three minutes! The final of the 1899–1900 Birmingham Senior Cup was abandoned through bad light with just ten minutes to go. Wolves were leading Burslem Port Vale 2–1 but thankfully the result was allowed to stand. Playing at Leeds United on 12 December 1936, Wolves lost centre-half Stan Cullis with a broken collar bone and had goalkeeper Alex Scott sent-off. The match was abandoned through fog with just seven minutes remaining and Wolves leading. The replay on 21 April 1937 saw Wolves win 1–0. On Boxing Day 1962, Wolves were leading West Bromwich Albion 2–0 in the local derby when the game was abandoned. In the rearranged fixture on 16 March 1963, Wolves won 7–0, scoring five times in the last quarter of the match.

**ADDENBROOKE, JACK** Jack Addenbrooke was associated with Wolverhampton Wanderers for almost 40 years after joining the club as a reserve team player during the 1880s whilst working as a teacher in a local school. In August 1885 he was appointed the club's secretary-manager, though at the time he did not have full powers of team selection nor complete control over which players the club were to sign. During Addenbrooke's time in charge the club had an excellent FA Cup record, for after losing to Preston North End 3–0 in the 1889 final at the Oval, they won the Cup in 1893 when they beat Everton 1–0 at Fallowfield. Two years later they reached the final again only to lose to Sheffield Wednesday but in 1908 were once more victorious when they beat Newcastle United 3–1. In 1921, Wolves reached the final for a fifth time under Addenbrooke but lost 1–0 to Tottenham Hotspur at Stamford Bridge. Addenbrooke was also the Staffordshire FA vice-president, serving on the committee for 28 years from 1894. In 1909 he was awarded the Football League long-service medal.

**AEROPLANE PROBLEMS** An aeroplane was chartered to fly Bill Slater, a member of the staff of Birmingham University in the early 1950s and part-time professional with the Molineux club, to an evening match against Sheffield Wednesday at Hillsborough. The Auster pilot was unable to locate the landing strip and when the aircraft did come down unheralded at the RAF Aerodrome at Worksop, it was surrounded by ambulances, fire engines and angry officers. Wolves kicked off that evening, and Slater was still trying to hitch a lift to the ground.

**AGGREGATE SCORE** Wolverhampton Wanderer's highest aggregate score in any competition came in the 1971–72 UEFA Cup when they beat both Academica Coimbra and FC Den Haag by an aggregate scoreline of 7–1. Against Academica Coimbra in the first round second leg, Derek Dougan netted a hat-trick in a 4–1 win after Wolves had won 3–0 in Portugal. After beating FC Den Haag 3–1 in Holland, Wolves won 4–0 in the second leg in front of a Molineux crowd of 20,299 with three Dutch players each scoring an own goal!

**ALLEN, HARRY** One of the club's greatest players, Harry Allen began his career with his home town club Walsall Swifts before joining Wolverhampton Wanderers in 1886. His first game was an FA Cup tie against Matlock on 30 October 1886 which Wolves won 6–0. He appeared in two FA Cup finals for Wolves as they lost 3–0 to Preston North End in 1889 and beat Everton 1–0 in 1893 when he scored the Wolves' goal. The centre-half also won five caps for England whilst with Wolves, the first against Wales in 1887–88. He played in the club's first Football League game on 8 September 1888 as Wolves drew 1–1 with Aston Villa and was ever-present as they finished in third place in the inaugural season of league football. He went on to play in 153 League and Cup games for the club, scoring 13 goals before injury and illness forced him to hang up his boots. He then worked as a coalman and a licensee before dying at the tragically young age of 29.

**ALLEN, RONNIE** Ronnie Allen was soon finding the net for his local side Port Vale and in 1947-48, his first full season, he was the club's top scorer with 13 goals including hat-tricks in the wins over Aldershot and Watford. He had scored 38 goals in 135 League and Cup games when in March 1950 he was allowed to join West Bromwich Albion for £20,000. He scored on his Albion début in a 1-1 draw at home to Wolves and, over the next 11 seasons, scored 231 goals in 457 first-team appearances. At the Hawthorns, Allen won five full caps for England and in 1954 won an FA Cup medal as the Baggies beat Preston North End 3–2. In May 1961 he joined Crystal Palace and scored 37 goals in 109 games for the Selhurst Park club before retiring. He then became coach of Wolverhampton Wanderers, taking over as manager on Andy Beattie's departure in January 1966. When Allen took over, Wolves were struggling near the foot of the Second Division but he bought wisely, signing both Mike Bailey and Derek Dougan, and in 1966–67 they won promotion to the First Division. When things started to go wrong at Molineux, Allen was sacked and spent four years abroad managing Athletico Bilbao and Sporting Lisbon. After returning to England to take charge at Walsall, he returned to the Hawthorns, first as scouting adviser and then as manager. He later took charge of the Saudi Arabia national side and Panathinaikos of Athens before returning to manage West Bromwich Albion for a second time.

**ANGLO–ITALIAN CUP** When Swindon Town won the Football League Cup in 1969 they were ineligible for the Fairs Cup because they were not a First Division side. Consequently, they organised a match against the Italian League Cup winners AS Roma, playing for the Anglo-Italian League Cup. The following year, the Anglo-Italian Cup was introduced for club sides from the two countries who had no involvement in Europe. Wolves entered the competition in May 1970, but despite winning three of their four games, they failed to qualify from their group after losing a physical match at Lazio, when a draw would have seen them through. Their results were:

| | | |
|---|---|---|
| Fiorentina | Home 2–1 | Away 3–1 |
| Lazio | Home 1–0 | Away 0–2 |

Wolves next entered the competition when it was reintroduced in 1992–93. Their results were:

| | |
|---|---|
| Tranmere Rovers | Away 1–2 |
| Peterborough United | Home 2–0 |

The club fared little better in 1993–94, again failing to qualify for the knockout stages.

| | |
|---|---|
| Stoke City | Home 3–3 |
| Birmingham City | Away 2–2 |

The club last entered the competition in 1994–95 when it was organised along different lines with Wolves playing Italian teams in the international stage. Their results were:

| | |
|---|---|
| Lecce | Away 1–0 |
| Ascoli | Home 0–1 |
| Venezia | Away 1–2 |
| Atalanta | Home 1–1 |

**ANNIS, WALTER** Hard-tackling half-back Walter Annis joined Wolves from Stafford Road in the summer of 1898. After making his début in a 2–0 win at Bury in March 1899, he had to wait until the 1900–01 season before establishing himself in the first team. He formed an outstanding half-back line with Ted Pheasant and George Fleming and then towards the end of his seven seasons with the club with Jack Whitehouse and George Walker. Annis, who appeared in 147 League and Cup games for Wolves, scored just one goal and that came on 25 March 1901 to secure a point for the Molineux club in a 1–1 draw at Sheffield United. Annis left Wolves to play for Cradley Heath in 1905.

**APPEARANCES** Derek Parkin holds the record for the highest number of League and Cup appearances in a Wolverhampton Wanderers shirt, with a total of 609 games to his credit between 1968 and 1982. The players with the highest number of appearances are as follows:

| | League | FA Cup | Lg Cup | Others | Total |
|---|---|---|---|---|---|
| 1. Derek Parkin | 500(1) | 45(1) | 35 | 27 | 607(2) |
| 2. Kenny Hibbitt | 447(19) | 46(1) | 35(1) | 24(1) | 552(22) |
| 3. Billy Wright | 490 | 48 | 0 | 3 | 541 |
| 4. Steve Bull | 450(9) | 18(2) | 30(1) | 33(1) | 531(13) |
| 5. Ron Flowers | 467 | 31 | 0 | 14 | 512 |
| 6. Peter Broadbent | 452 | 31 | 0 | 14 | 497 |
| 7. John McAlle | 394(12) | 43(1) | 27 | 31 | 495(13) |
| 8. Geoff Palmer | 410(6) | 38(1) | 33 | 8 | 489(7) |
| 9. Jimmy Mullen | 445 | 38 | 0 | 3 | 486 |
| 10. John Richards | 365(20) | 42(2) | 32(1) | 22(2) | 461(25) |

**ASSAULT** Wolves' Northern Ireland international Derek Dougan got a nasty shock when he scored a last-minute equaliser for the Molineux club against Millwall in their Second Division match in April 1967. As he turned to celebrate with a fan who had rushed on to the pitch, he was promptly punched in the face – the fan was a Millwall supporter!

**ATKINS, MARK** England schoolboy international Mark Atkins began his Football League career with Scunthorpe United and had appeared in 66 first team games for the Irons when Blackburn Rovers paid £45,000 for his services in the summer of 1988. The midfielder was a virtual ever-present in seven seasons at Ewood Park, helping the club win the Premier League title in 1994–5. He had scored 40 goals in 312 games for Rovers when in September 1995 he signed for Wolves for a fee of £1 million. Booked on his début in a goalless home draw against Luton Town, he was moved from midfield to the sweeper position during the 1996–97 season with great effect before being restored to a more forward position. He has continued to show his versatility and in 1997–98 captained the club in a number of games during Keith Curle's absence. At the time of writing, Atkins has appeared in 135 first team games for the Molineux club.

**ATTENDANCE – AVERAGE** The average home league attendance of Wolverhampton Wanderers over the last ten seasons have been as follows:

| | | | |
|---|---|---|---|
| 1988–89 | 14,392 | 1993–94 | 22,008 |
| 1989–90 | 17,045 | 1994–95 | 25,940 |
| 1990–91 | 15,837 | 1995–96 | 24,786 |
| 1991–92 | 13,743 | 1996–97 | 24,763 |
| 1992–93 | 13,598 | 1997–98 | 23,281 |

**ATTENDANCE – HIGHEST** The record attendance at Molineux is 61,315 for the fifth round FA Cup game with Liverpool on 11 February 1939. The match ended in a 4–1 win for Wolves with goals from Burton, Dorsett, McIntosh and Westcott.

**ATTENDANCE – LOWEST** The lowest attendance at Molineux is just 900 for the visit of Notts County in a First Division game on 17 October 1891. For the record, Wolves won 2–1 with goals from internationals Jack Bowdler (Wales) and Dick Topham (England).

**AWAY MATCHES** Wolverhampton Wanderers' best away win came in the Football League on 3 September 1955 when they won 9–1 against Cardiff City at Ninian Park. Wolves have also won three away matches by a 7–1 scoreline against Ashington in 1923–24; Port Vale in 1931–32; and Huddersfield Town in 1951–52. Wolves' worst defeat away from home is 10–1 by Newton Heath on 15 October 1892. The club also conceded ten goals in 1919–20 when they lost 10–3 to Hull City at Boothferry Park.

**AWAY SEASONS** The club's highest number of away wins came in 1958–59 when they won 13 of their 21 matches in winning the League Championship. The club failed to win an away game in seasons 1895–96 and 1992–93 when they finished bottom of Division Two and were relegated to the Third Division (North) for the first time in their history.

# B

**BADDELEY, TOM** Goalkeeper Tom Baddeley played his early football for his local sides, Burslem Swifts and Burslem Port Vale, where he was ever-present in seasons 1894–95 and 1895–96. However, he was suspended in August 1896 after signing a second professional form for another club! In October 1896 he was sold to Wolverhampton Wanderers for £50 but didn't make his début until the opening game of the following season when Wolves beat Preston North End 3–0. Though he only stood 5ft 9ins, he was more than capable of standing up to the burly forwards of the day, who would attempt to bundle him and the ball over the line. Baddeley was very agile and able to deal with any kind of shot. He could also throw the ball out 50 yards which was unusual in those days. Capped by England on five occasions whilst with Wolves, he spent 11 seasons at Molineux and appeared in 315 games before leaving to sign for Bradford Park Avenue. After ending his league career with Stoke at the end of the 1913–14 season, he played non-league football for Whitfield Colliery.

**BAILEY, MIKE** One of the club's greatest servants, Mike Bailey played his early football with non-league Gorleston before being signed by Charlton Athletic in the summer of 1958. He turned professional in March 1959 and made his league début for the London club the following Christmas. His performances for Charlton led to his winning five England Under-23 caps and two at full level, as he developed into one of the best wing-halves in the country. Bailey, who was also Charlton's captain, broke a leg in the match against Middlesbrough in October 1964 but recovered well to play in a total of 169 games before joining Wolves for £40,000 in March 1966. He made his début in a 1–1 home draw against Southampton and appeared in the final 11 games of the season

*Mike Bailey*

before helping Wolves win promotion to the First Division in
1966–67. That season, Bailey was voted 'Midland Footballer of the
Year'. When Wolves reached the final of the 1972 UEFA Cup
against Spurs, Bailey was on the bench but skippered the side to
victory against Manchester City in the League Cup final of 1974.

When he left Wolves in the summer of 1977, he had scored 25 goals in 436 games for the club. He joined Minnesota Kicks in the NASL for £15,000 before later becoming player-coach of Hereford United and then manager of Charlton Athletic. At The Valley he was appointed too late to prevent their relegation to Division Three but the following season they bounced straight back again, promoted in third place. After his move to Brighton, where he helped steer the club to 13th in the First Division, he went to coach abroad.

**BARNES, DAVID** Paddington-born full-back David Barnes began his career with Coventry City where he won 14 England youth caps. Unable to win a regular first-team place at Highfield Road, he moved to Ipswich Town but injuries and a loss of form limited his appearances to 17 in just over two seasons with the Suffolk club. He joined Wolves for a fee of £35,000 in October 1984 and made his début in a 3–2 defeat at Notts County that month. Though his first two seasons with the club saw Wolves suffer successive relegations, Barnes was a virtual ever-present. He went on to score four goals in 107 games from his position at left-back before joining Aldershot for £25,000 in the summer of 1987. He moved to Sheffield United two years later and helped the Bramall Lane club win promotion to the Premier League in 1991–92. He had made 106 first-team appearances for the Blades when in January 1994 they sold him to Watford for £50,000. Suffering from injuries and unable to settle at Vicarage Road, he was given a free transfer and joined Colchester United where he played out his league career.

**BARNWELL, JOHN** An amateur with the famous Bishop Auckland team, John Barnwell attracted the attention of a number of Football League clubs before signing for Arsenal in November 1956. It was whilst doing his National Service in the RASC that he was chosen to represent the British Army. At Highbury he made 151 league and cup appearances and won one England Under-23 cap. He joined Nottingham Forest in March 1964 for £30,000 and as one of the game's first true midfield players, settled into a deep-lying linking role. In six seasons at the City Ground he scored 25 goals in 201 league and Cup appearances. He was transferred to Sheffield United at the end of the 1969–70 season but soon left to become coach at Hereford United and later Peterborough United. In November 1979, Barnwell was named as Wolves' new manager after a week of speculation. The Molineux club almost made it to Wembley that season but lost in the FA Cup semi-final to one of his former clubs, Arsenal. Barnwell almost lost his life in a horrific car crash in which he suffered a fractured skull. He returned to take charge just after the start of the 1979–80 season and set the football world talking when he sold Steve Daley to Manchester City for £1.15 million and brought Andy Gray to Molineux from Aston Villa for £1.5 million. It was the Scottish international who scored Wolves' goal when they beat Nottingham Forest 1–0 to win the League Cup in 1980. The following season, Wolves reached the FA Cup semi-finals but finished 18th in the First Division. With Wolves bottom of the league in January 1982, Barnwell was given an ultimatum, to accept the terms of a new contract or resign. Not surprisingly he terminated his contract after seeking legal advice and after a spell coaching in Saudi Arabia, he became manager of AEK Athens. He later returned to this country and managed both Notts County and Walsall.

**BARRACLOUGH, BILLY** Outside-left Billy Barraclough began his career with Bridlington Town before joining Hull City. Though he had made only nine appearances in the Yorkshire club's Second Division side of 1927–28, Wolves brought him to Molineux where his speed made him one of the club's most effective wingers. His first game in the gold and black of Wolves was a 3–2 home win over Clapton Orient in December 1928 and though he made only three appearances in that campaign, the following season saw him establish himself as a first team regular. During the club's Second Division championship-winning season of 1931–32, Barraclough scored seven goals in 40 games. The two games he missed were due to him having to serve a two-week suspension after being sent off in a 2–1 defeat at Stoke City. When he left Molineux to join Chelsea for a fee of £1,500 in October 1934, he had scored 19 goals in 183 league and cup games for Wolves. At Stamford Bridge, the stocky winger scored 11 goals in 81 games but after being barracked by a section of the Chelsea crowd, he left to play for Colchester United before ending his career with Doncaster Rovers.

**BAUGH, DICKY Sen.** England international full-back Dicky Baugh joined Wolves from Stafford Road FC in May 1886 and was a regular member of the side for eight seasons following the club's entry into the Football League. His two international caps came four years apart, Baugh winning his first against Ireland in 1886 when England won 6–1 in Belfast and then in 1890 against the same opposition at the same venue when England triumphed 9–1. He won an FA Cup winners' medal in 1893 as Wolves beat Everton 1–0 and appeared in two other FA Cup finals for the club in 1889 and 1896 but was on the losing side on both occasions. Strong in the tackle and a good distributor of the ball, he appeared in over 200 games for the Molineux club before leaving in September 1896 to end his career with Walsall.

**BAUGH, DICKY Jun.** Dicky Baugh's son joined Wolves in the summer of 1918 and turned professional some 12 months later. His first league game in Wolves' colours was in a 1–0 home defeat by Bury in October 1919 but by the turn of the year, he had established himself as a first-team regular in the Molineux club's side. Sadly, the hard-tackling full-back missed the club's appearance in the 1921 FA Cup final through injury. Soon afterwards he was induced by an agent to join Cardiff City but an FA/Welsh FA Commission investigated the deal and found it to be illegal. As a result, Baugh was fined £20 and the Welsh club £50. He continued to play for Wolves and had made 120 appearances when in the summer of 1924 he joined West Bromwich Albion. He made 65 appearances for the Baggies before joining Exeter City and later ending his career with non-league Kidderminster Harriers.

**BAYNTON, JACK** One of the great names in the early history of the club, Jack Baynton was a pupil-teacher at St Luke's School and along with his best friend Jack Brodie, helped to form Wolverhampton Wanderers. For St Luke's, Baynton acted at different times as club captain, secretary and treasurer and from here he left to 'join' Wolves in 1877. A fine utility player, appearing at both centre-half and inside-right, he eventually became the club's goalkeeper and was between the posts during their first season in the Football League in 1888–89. At the end of that campaign he played his last match for the club in the 3–0 defeat by Preston North End in the FA Cup final at The Kennington Oval. Legend has it that he once scored a goal from fully 100 yards in a local cup game at Dudley Road! He later became a teacher at All Saints School in Hockley, Birmingham and took up refereeing, officiating in a number of first-class matches.

**BEATS, BILLY** Centre-forward Billy Beats played his early football with Port Hill and Port Vale Rovers before establishing himself with Burslem Port Vale. In 1893–94, his second season with the club, he was the top scorer. Playing in every match, Beats scored 20 goals including hat-tricks in a 5–0 home win over Small Heath and the 6–4 Staffordshire Cup defeat against Wolverhampton Wanderers. It was that performance that led to the Molineux club signing Beats and he made his Wolverhampton début in the opening game of the 1895–96 season, scoring one of the goals in a 5–1 win over Burnley. He ended that season with 14 goals and played in the FA Cup final where Wolves lost 2–1 to Sheffield Wednesday. He was the club's top scorer for the next two seasons and went on to score 73 goals in 218 games. His form towards the end of his eight seasons at Molineux led to him winning two full international caps, the first against Wales in May 1901. He left Molineux in the summer of 1903 to join Bristol Rovers but three years later, after captaining them to the Southern League Championship, he returned to the Potteries to play for Port Vale. He top-scored for the Valiants in 1906–07 but at the end of the campaign he was released as the club faced a financial crisis. Beats, who had scored 43 goals in 117 games during his two spells with the club, left to end his career with Reading, where he later became trainer.

**BEATTIE, ANDY** A Scottish international, he has probably been involved with more clubs than any other person in the history of English football. He began his League career with Preston North End and appeared for the Lilywhites in the 1937 and 1938 FA Cup finals. He won seven Scottish caps between April 1937 and December 1938 plus another five in wartime internationals. On retirement from playing, Beattie's first managerial position was with Barrow but after producing a new-found team spirit he had a disagreement with the club chairman. He resigned but was reinstated when the other directors forced the chairman to leave instead. After moving to Stockport County in a similar capacity, he was enticed to Huddersfield Town in April 1952 and, although he was too late to stave off relegation, he guided them to promotion the following season. He served twice as team manager of Scotland, once in 1954 when he took them to the World Cup finals, and for a brief period in 1959–60. After resigning at Huddersfield in 1956 he had a short spell with Carlisle United before replacing Billy Walker at Nottingham Forest. Beattie spent three seasons at the City Ground before joining Plymouth Argyle as caretaker-manager and saved them from relegation by the slimmest of margins. In November 1964, Beattie was appointed caretaker-manager of Wolverhampton Wanderers, taking over from the legendary Stan Cullis. During his first season at the club he used 28 players and the campaign ended in relegation to the Second Division. After a 9–3 defeat at Southampton and the illness of his wife, Beattie decided that he had had enough and resigned. In December 1965 he joined Notts County as general manager and later had coaching and scouting spells with Sheffield United, Brentford, Wolves, Walsall and Liverpool. Enjoying a long, successful career in the game, he left his mark on many clubs in the Football League.

**BELL, NORMAN** 'Super-sub' Norman Bell joined Wolves as an apprentice in the summer of 1971 before turning professional in November 1973. After making his début in a goalless home draw against Aston Villa in September 1975, he went on to appear in 100 games in the next six seasons, 28 of them as a substitute. His versatility – for Bell was equally effective as a striker or in midfield – made him the ideal choice to have on the bench. He left Molineux in November 1981 and joined Blackburn Rovers. He spent three seasons at Ewood Park, scoring 10 goals in 61 league games before entering non-league football as player-manager of local side, Darwen.

**BELLAMY, GARY** Gary Bellamy began his career with Chesterfield where he made 207 first team appearances and helped the Spireites win the Fourth Division Championship in 1984–85. He joined Wolves in the summer of 1987 for a bargain fee of £17,000 and made his début in a 2–2 draw at home to Crewe Alexandra on 12 September 1987. He soon established himself in the Wolves' defence and helped the club win the Fourth Division Championship in his first season. Also that season he was a member of the Wolves side that beat Burnley in the final of the Sherpa Van Trophy and in 1988–89 won a Third Division Championship medal. Bellamy, who had a loan spell with Cardiff City towards the end of the 1991–92 season, made 164 first–team appearances before leaving Molineux in September 1992 to join Leyton Orient for a fee of £30,000. The vastly experienced defender served Orient well for four seasons but

*George Berry*

in the summer of 1996, after he had played in 155 games, he was released.

**BERRY, GEORGE** Despite being born in Rostrop, West Germany, George Berry went on to play for Wales at full international level, winning five caps between May 1979 and February 1983. He made his Football League début for Wolves in a vital promotion clash against Chelsea at Molineux on 7 May 1977 in a game that ended all-square at 1–1. However, it was 1978–79 before he established himself as first-team regular and over the next four seasons he went on to take his total of league and cup appearances for Wolves to 160. In 1980 he won a league Cup winners' medal as the Molineux club beat Nottingham Forest 1–0 in the final. In the summer of 1982, Berry joined Stoke City and within a short period had been made team captain. He was to stay at the Victoria Ground for eight seasons and despite loan spells at Doncaster Rovers and a brief sojourn in Portuguese football, Berry amassed a total of 269 first-team appearances for the Potters. He then joined Peterborough United and in his only season captained the club to promotion from the Fourth Division. He then signed for Preston North End but as his legs could not stand the pressure of playing home games on plastic, he was loaned to Aldershot where he ended his league career.

**BEST STARTS** Wolverhampton Wanderers were unbeaten for the first 12 games of both the 1949–50 and 1992–93 seasons. In 1949–50, Wolves won nine and drew three of their matches before losing 3–0 at Manchester United on 22 October 1949. The club ended the season as runners-up to Portsmouth in the First Division. In 1992–93, when the club finished 11th in the Endsleigh League Division One, they were once again undefeated in their opening 12 games, winning five and drawing seven. Their first defeat came at Millwall on 25 October 1992 when they went down 2–0.

**BETTELEY, DICK** Full-back Dick Betteley joined Wolves from his home town club Bilston United in the summer of 1900. After turning professional the following year, he made his league début for the Molineux club in March 1902. Forming an outstanding full-back pairing with Jack Jones, he went on to appear in 123 first-team games over the next four seasons. His only goal for the club came in the 3–1 home defeat by Stoke in April 1905. Betteley left Wolves at the end of the 1905–06 season to join West Bromwich Albion and though he struggled at times to win a regular first-team place, he helped the Throstles win the Second Division Championship in 1911–12. He had played in 89 games for Albion before returning to see out his career with Bilston United.

**BIRCH, PAUL** The right-sided midfielder was a member of the Aston Villa FA Youth Cup-winning side of 1980, the year he turned professional. He made his first team début in a 1–0 home win over Sunderland in August 1983. Over the next eight seasons, he scored 24 goals in 212 League and Cup appearances for the Villans, helping them win promotion to the First Division in 1987–88. In January 1991, Wolves paid £400,000 to take him to Molineux and after scoring on his début in a 2–1 home win over West Ham United, Birch went on to give the club good service. Sadly, towards the end of the 1993–94 season, he began to suffer from a series of niggling injuries which resulted in him losing his first-team place. He had scored 19 goals in 168 first-team games for Wolves before joining Preston North End on loan. He then played for Doncaster Rovers, later signing for Exeter City on a free transfer.

**BISHOP, ALF** Alf Bishop played his early football with Halesowen before signing for Wolves in the summer of 1905. Able to play in any of the three half-back positions, he initially occupied the centre-half spot for Wolves in his first couple of seasons with the club before switching to wing-half. Over the next ten seasons, Bishop missed only a handful of games and was ever-present in seasons 1906–07, 1909–10, 1910–11 and 1914–15. He won an FA Cup winners' medal in 1908 as Wolves beat Newcastle United 3–1. During the First World War he 'guested' for Merthyr Town but when football resumed after the hostilities, he returned to Molineux to play in 31 league games during the 1919–20 season. At the end of that campaign, which had seen him take his club total of appearances to 382, he left the Midlands club and joined Wrexham. Though he played a number of games for the Welsh club in the Birmingham and District League, he never appeared for the Robins in the Football League after they were admitted to the Third Division (North) in 1921–22.

**BLACK, DAVID** Winger David Black started his career with Rovers FC and Hurlford with whom he had played for Scotland against Ireland in March 1889. He then played for Grimsby Town in their first two seasons in the Football Alliance and then followed that with two years at Middlesbrough. Whilst with 'Boro, who at that time were members of the Northern League, Black scored against Wolves in a 2–1 win for the Molineux club in the FA Cup competition of

1892–93. He joined Wolves in July 1893 and made his début at Nottingham Forest on the opening day of the 1893–94 season as Wolves were beaten 7–1. The following season he played most of his games at inside-left but in 1895–96 he reverted to outside-left and scored 11 goals in 30 League and Cup outings including Wolves' goal in the 2–1 FA Cup final defeat by Sheffield Wednesday at The Crystal Palace. He had scored 17 goals in 83 games for Wolves when he left to join Burnley in December 1896. After netting five goals in 12 games he was on the move again, this time to Tottenham Hotspur where he proved to be a great success, scoring 25 goals in 56 first-team games. At the end of the 1897–98 season he moved to Woolwich Arsenal but had little opportunity to establish himself before joining Clyde.

**BLACKETT, JOE** Left-back Joe Blackett began his football career with his home-town club Newcastle United before later playing for Gateshead and Loughborough Town. He joined Wolves in May 1897 and made his first team début in a 3–0 home win over Preston North End on the opening day of the 1897–98 season. He went on to be an ever-present in his first season with the club as Wolves finished third in the First Division. In the last game of that campaign, Blackett scored the first of 12 goals in a 5–0 demolition of Sheffield Wednesday and in 1898–99, when he had a short spell at inside-left, he scored five goals in two games including a hat-trick in a 4–1 home win over Sheffield United. He went on to appear in 103 League and Cup games for the Molineux club before leaving in April 1900 to join Derby County. Illness marred his time at the Baseball Ground as it did with his future clubs, Middlesbrough, Luton and Leicester Fosse. Blackett also had a spell as player-manager of Rochdale, whom he led to the Lancashire Combination Championship, and played for Barrow before becoming Reading's trainer.

**BOOTH, COLIN** Middleton-born inside-forward Colin Booth played for Manchester Schoolboys in the final of the English Schools Trophy, captained the Lancashire Schoolboys County FA Representative side and was an England Schoolboy international trialist. He joined Wolves as a junior in the summer of 1950, turning professional in January 1952. However, he had to wait until 11 April 1955 before making his first-team début in a 1–0 home win over Aston Villa. The following season saw Booth become a regular member of the Wolves side and in the final game of the campaign at Sheffield United, he scored a hat-trick in a 3–3 draw. In 1956–57 he scored four goals as Wolves beat Arsenal at Molineux 5–2 and the following two seasons helped them win the League Championship. However, despite his goalscoring he was never an automatic choice and in October 1959, after scoring 27 goals in 82 games, he joined Nottingham Forest for a fee of £20,000. Capped by England at Under-23 level, Booth scored 39 goals in 87 league games for Forest before joining Doncaster Rovers. He appeared in 88 games for the Belle Vue club before moving to Oxford United in July 1964 for what was then a record fee of £7,500 for the Manor Ground club. Sadly, Colin Booth was forced to retire through injury at the end of the 1966–67 season.

**BOTTRILL, WALTER** Goalscoring inside-forward Walter Bottrill began his professional career with Middlesbrough but after two seasons at Ayresome Park, he moved to Nelson. He helped the Lancashire club to runners-up spot in the Third Division (North) before playing for Rotherham United and then York City. In his only season at Bootham Crescent he was the club's top scorer and netted a hat-trick against Wigan Borough. Bottrill joined Wolves in the summer of 1930 and played his first game for the club in a 4–3 win at Nottingham Forest on the opening day of the 1930–31 season. The following season he formed a prolific goalscoring partnership with Billy Hartill as Wolves won the Second Division Championship. Bottrill scored 21 goals in 38 games and the two players between them netted 60 of the club's 115 goals. Towards the end of the following season, he parted company with the club after scoring 44 goals in 109 outings and signed for Huddersfield Town. He later joined Chesterfield but, after failing to break into their first team, hung up his boots after scoring 105 goals in 314 games for his six league clubs.

**BOWEN, TOMMY** Tommy Bowen began his league career with Walsall where he scored 17 goals in 81 games before joining Wolves in March 1924. After making his début in a 1–1 draw at Wigan Borough, he scored on his first appearance at Molineux as Wolves beat Tranmere Rovers 3–0 and appeared in the last four games of the club's Third Division (North) Championship-winning season. Bowen formed an effective striking partnership with Tom Phillipson and Harry Lees and in 94 games for the club scored 24 goals with a best of eight in 27 games in 1924–25. On leaving Molineux in the summer of 1928, Bowen joined Coventry but after making only 17 appearances in two seasons, left to play non–league football with Kidderminster Harriers.

**BRADSHAW, PAUL** Goalkeeper Paul Bradshaw had trials with Manchester United before joining Blackburn Rovers where he won England Youth honours during his time at Ewood Park. He had appeared in 78 league games for the Lancashire club when he became Wolves' record signing in September 1977 as Sammy Chung paid £150,000 for his services. He made his début in a 3–0 home win over Leicester City, a match in which John Richards scored a hat-trick and kept his place in the side for the remaining 34 games. In fact, Bradshaw remained a regular in the Welsh side for five seasons before losing his place to John Burridge. By the time he left Molineux, he had appeared in 243 first-team games, won a League Cup winners' medal and represented England Under-23s on four occasions. After a spell in the NASL with Vancouver Whitecaps, he returned to England and joined West Bromwich Albion. He had spells as a non-contract player with Bristol Rovers and Newport County but when the Welsh club folded, he joined Peterborough United where he took his total of Football League appearances to 359.

**BRIBES** Newspaper allegations that Wolverhampton Wanderers players were offered bribes to lose their match with Leeds United which decided the League Championship in 1972 were referred to the Director of Public Prosecutions. The Leeds chairman strongly denied the claims.

**BROADBENT, PETER** Inside-forward Peter Broadbent joined Brentford as a professional from Dover FC in the summer of 1950 but after just 16 league outings for the Bees, he left Griffin Park to join Wolverhampton Wanderers for £10,000 in February 1951. Manager Stan Cullis gave him his début in the home game against Portsmouth the following month and though he impressed, the Fratton Park club won 3–2. Over the next 14 seasons, Broadbent went on to give Wolves great service both as a goal-maker and a goalscorer. He won three League Championship medals in seasons

*Paul Bradshaw*

1953–54, 1957–58 and 1958–59 and an FA Cup winners' medal in 1960 as Wolves beat Blackburn Rovers 3–0. He won seven full caps for England, the first against the Soviet Union in the World Cup finals of 1958. His only goals at full international level came when he scored both England goals in a 2–2 draw with Wales at Villa Park in November 1958. His best season for Wolves in terms of goals scored was 1958–59 when he top-scored with 22 goals including a hat-trick in a 5–3 win at Portsmouth. He went on to score 145 goals in 497 games before leaving Wolves for Shrewsbury Town in January 1965. He later played for Aston Villa and Stockport County before ending his career playing non-league football for Bromsgrove Rovers.

**BRODIE, JACK** After helping to form Wolverhampton Wanderers in 1877, Jack Brodie continued to serve the club as a player until retiring at the end of the 1890–91 season. Though he could play in a variety of positions, Brodie was the club's leading scorer for the first five years of competitive football, his first goal coming in the FA Cup victory over Long Eaton Rangers in October 1883. His pace and powerful shooting were just two of the qualities that led to his winning the first of three full caps for England in March 1889; he scored in a 6–1 win over Ireland. That season he appeared for Wolves in the FA Cup final but was bitterly disappointed as their opponents Preston North End won 3–0. After scoring 44 goals in 65 League and Cup games he hung up his boots and took up refereeing which he did outwith his teaching role as assistant-headmaster at St Peter's School, Wolverhampton. In 1913 he was voted on to the club's board of directors.

**BROOKS, SAMMY** As a boy, Sammy Brooks played local junior football for Brierley Hill Alliance until joining Bilston United as a 16-year-old where he was spotted by Wolverhampton Wanderers. He was initially associated with the Molineux club as an amateur but within two years of signing professional forms, he was the established first-choice left-winger. He made his début in a goalless home draw against Bradford Park Avenue in April 1911. His best season for the club in terms of goals scored was 1914–15 when he came second in the scoring charts with 18 goals in 37 league outings. While with Wolves he represented the Football League against the Irish League in October 1914; played for England against Wales in a 1919–20 Victory International; and appeared in the 1921 FA Cup final against Tottenham Hotspur at Stamford Bridge. Brooks had scored 54 goals in 250 games for Wolves when he moved to Tottenham Hotspur in the summer of 1922. Sadly he was a disappointment at White Hart Lane, scoring three goals in 16 games during his two years with the London club. He was placed on the transfer list but as no club came in for him, he played for Birmingham League Kidderminster, with Spurs retaining his Football League registration until a transfer to Southend United. He later played for Cradley Heath and Stourbridge.

**BROTHERS** There have been a number of instances of brothers playing for Wolverhampton Wanderers. One of the earliest instances was in the club's pre-league days when Jack and Harry Aston represented the club in a number of FA Cup ties although they never played in the same Wolves side. In 1927–28 Reg and Walter Weaver played in a number of matches together but it was Reg, who went on to score 29 goals in 51 games, who was the more prominent player. Scottish inside-forwards Jimmy and Richard Deacon played for Wolves in the late 1920s and early 1930s. Jimmy Deacon scored 56 goals in 158 games, whilst Richard's three first-team appearances were as a replacement for his injured brother, so they never played on the same Wolves' side. Dai and Billy Richards played together for Wolves but Dai, who scored five goals in 229 games, was the better player. Yorkshire-born brothers Jack and Frank Taylor were full-back partners for Wolves before the Second World War and in June 1952 they both became managers for the first time within a week of each other. During 1960–61 they both lost their jobs, Jack at Leeds and Frank at Stoke City. Wayne and Derek Clarke were members of the famous footballing family whose brother Allan played 19 times for England. Whilst Wayne scored 33 goals in 170 games for the Molineux club, brother Derek appeared in just five games before going on to appear in 178 league games for Oxford United. On 17 February 1973 in a Division One match, Wolves drew 1–1 with Newcastle United at Molineux. Kenny Hibbitt put Wolves ahead in the first half and his brother Terry Hibbitt equalised after the interval!

**BUCKLEY, FRANK** Although Major Frank Buckley is one of the most famous managers of all time, none of his sides won a major honour, although Wolves came close to the league and cup double in 1939 but *just* missed out on both. Born in Urmston, Buckley served as a player with Aston Villa, Brighton, Manchester United, Manchester City, Birmingham, Derby County and Bradford City before the First World War, winning one England cap against Ireland in 1914. He had fought in the Boer War and in World War One he joined the 17th Middlesex Regiment as an officer, reaching the rank of major in 1916. He commanded the 'Footballers' Battalion', made up of soccer professionals, and on his return continued to be known as Major Buckley. After the hostilities he became manager of Norwich City but due to a crisis at the club, six directors resigned, many players left and Buckley also resigned. After a spell in charge at Blackpool, he was appointed manager of Wolverhampton Wanderers. By the time the Second World War came, Wolves had risen from a mediocre Second Division side to runners-up in the League and FA Cup. In his early years with the club Buckley signed some outstanding players, notably Walter Bottrill, Charlie Phillips, Dai Richards and Alf Tootill and in 1931–32 the club returned to the top flight after winning the Second Division Championship. In the 1930s, Buckley brought players of the calibre of Stan Cullis, Billy Wright, Jimmy Mullen and Dennis Westcott to Molineux and they were just about to reach their peak when the war came. After finishing runners-up in the First Division to Everton in 1938-39 they were surprisingly beaten 4–1 by Second Division Portsmouth in the FA Cup final. Though some of Buckley's methods were deemed controversial, like his monkey-gland injections, they were in reality just inoculations against colds. However, he did send a number of players to see a psychologist in his search for the elusive confidence that is so important to players. Buckley resigned his post in March 1944 following the retirement of his greatest ally, chairman Ben Matthews. He later managed Notts County, Hull City, Leeds United and Walsall before bowing out of the game at the age of 72.

**BULL, STEVE** The idol of Molineux, 'Bully' was given permission by West Bromwich Albion manager Ron Saunders to leave The Hawthorns in November 1986 for a mere £65,000 in a deal which also involved Andy Thompson. He immediately formed a deadly striking partnership with Andy Mutch and in 1986–87 Bull was the club's leading scorer with 15 goals in 30 league games including a

*Steve Bull*

hat-trick in a 4–1 win over Hartlepool United on the final day of the season. In 1987–88 Wolves won the Fourth Division Championship and Bull, in his first full season with the club, scored the remarkable total of 52 goals. He scored 34 of them in the league, including hat-tricks against Exeter City (Away 4–2) and Darlington (Home 5–3). In the Sherpa Van Trophy he scored in every round leading up to the final, where Wolves beat Burnley at Wembley – a total of 12 goals including another hat-trick in a 4–0 win over Brentford. In 1988–89 Bull scored 50 goals to become the first player for over 60 years to score over a hundred goals in consecutive English seasons. He scored 37 league goals as Wolves won the Third Division title including four in a 6–0 defeat of Preston North End and hat-tricks against Mansfield Town (Home 6–2), Fulham (Home 5–2) and Bury (Home 4–0). He also scored 11 goals in seven Sherpa Van Trophy matches including four in a 5–1 win over Port Vale and all three in the 3–0 defeat of Bristol City. Not surprisingly his goalscoring achievements brought him international recognition and after Under-21 and 'B' matches, he made his full début against Scotland at Hampden Park when he scored in a 2–0 win in May 1989. In 1989–90 Bull continued to find the back of the net with great regularity, scoring all four in a 4–1 win at Newcastle United and a hat-trick in a 5–0 home win over Leicester City. In 1990–91 he again topped the club's scoring charts, netting hat-tricks against Bristol City (Home 4–0) and Oxford United (Home 3–3). A further hat-trick followed against Derby County (Away 4–0) in 1993–94, whilst on the opening day of the 1996–97 season he scored his 17th hat-trick in a 3–1 win at Grimsby Town, a Wolves club record. Despite suffering from a series of injuries in recent seasons, Steve Bull remained a determined striker and at the time of writing he has scored a remarkable 300 goals in 544 first-team games. He has only just now (at the time of writing) annouced his retirement from the game.

**BUST** After Wolves were relegated from the First Division in 1981–82 they almost went out of existence. Rash spending to bring players to the club and £10 million for the new stand at Molineux left them over £2.5 million in debt at the end of that campaign. Then in early June 1982, Chesterfield issued the club with a writ for an outstanding instalment of a transfer fee. Within a couple of weeks, the Wolves' chairman had resigned and was replaced by Doug Ellis. The present Aston Villa chairman claimed that the Molineux club had been saved with a little over 24 hours to spare. However, the problems would not go away and early in July 1982, the Official Receiver was called in. Both the Football League and the Receiver set a deadline for attempts to rescue the ailing Molineux club and five consortia battled to try and raise the money before the end of the month. In the end Wolves were saved with just three minutes to spare by a group led by former Wolves and Northern Ireland international Derek Dougan.

# C

**CADDICK, BILL** Hard-tackling centre-half Bill Caddick began his career playing for his home-town team Wellington Town before signing professional forms for Wolves in December 1920. Signed as cover for Joe Hodnett, he made his début in a 1–0 defeat at Stoke and, though he only played in four games during that campaign, he got into the side on a regular basis at the start of the 1921–22 season. He was a virtual ever-present for the next five seasons, playing in 154 games including 36 in the club's Third Division (North) Championship-winning season of 1923–24. Caddick eventually lost his place to Sammy Charnley and, after one more season, he returned to Wellington Town where he finished his career.

**CAPACITY** The total capacity of Molineux in 1998–99 was 28,525.

**CAPS** The most-capped player in the club's history is Billy Wright who won 105 caps for England.

**CAPS (ENGLAND)** The first Wolverhampton Wanderers player to be capped by England was Charlie Mason, playing against Ireland in 1887. The most-capped player is Billy Wright with 105 caps.

**CAPS (NORTHERN IRELAND)** The first Wolverhampton Wanderers player to be capped by Northern Ireland was Billy Halligan when he played against England in 1912. The most-capped player is Derek Dougan with 26 caps.

**CAPS (REPUBLIC OF IRELAND)** The first Wolverhampton Wanderers player to be capped by the Republic of Ireland was David Jordan when he played against Switzerland in 1937. The most-capped player is Phil Kelly with five caps.

**CAPS (SCOTLAND)** The first Wolverhampton Wanderers player to be capped by Scotland was Hugh Curran when he played against Austria in 1969. The most-capped player is Andy Gray with 13 caps.

**CAPS (WALES)** The first Wolverhampton Wanderers player to be capped by Wales was Jack Bowdler when he played against Scotland in 1891. The most-capped player is Dai Richards with 11 caps.

**CAPTAINS** One of the club's earliest captains was Jack Baynton, a splendid utility player who didn't mind what position he played in as long as he was in the team. Harry Allen captained Wolves to their first FA Cup success in 1893, scoring the only goal of the game against Everton. Another of the club's early captains was Tom Baddeley, the England keeper who went on to appear in 315 games for Wolves. Billy Wooldridge captained Wolves when they next won the FA Cup in 1908 and had an outstanding match. Val Gregory, who later became Wolves' trainer, skippered the side in the 1921 FA Cup final against Tottenham Hotspur. When Wolves won the Second Division Championship in 1931–32 they were captained by full-back Wilf Lowton who scored nine goals from the penalty spot during that successful campaign. Charlie Phillips was captain when he was sent off in the 3–3 home draw against Bolton Wanderers at Christmas 1935. Stan Cullis became the youngest ever England captain when, on 26 October 1938 at the age of 22, he skippered the side against FIFA at Highbury. During the war years, Tom Galley captained Wolves when they won the League War Cup in 1942. Billy Wright captained Wolves to victory over Leicester City in the 1949 FA Cup final and to three League Championships in the 1950s as well as skippering England in 90 of his 105 international appearances. Bill Slater was the club's captain when they last won the FA Cup in 1960.

**CARR, WILLIE** Scottish international inside-forward Willie Carr began his career with Coventry City where he scored 33 goals in 252 league games during his eight years at Highfield Road. He joined Wolves in March 1985 for a fee of £80,000 and scored on his début in a 7–1 home win over Chelsea. He went on to suffer relegation to Division Two at the end of 1975–76 but then helped the club win the Second Division Championship at a canter in 1976–77. The period following promotion was another purple period in the history of Wolverhampton Wanderers, with the FA Cup semi-final being

*Willie Carr*

reached twice and the League Cup won over a three-year period. He went on to score 26 goals in 289 league and cup games before leaving to join Millwall in the summer of 1982. After only eight league appearances for the Lions, he moved into non-league football, playing for Worcester City, Willenhall Town and Stourbridge.

**CELEBRATIONS** When Peter Knowles headed a goal for Wolverhampton Wanderers at Portsmouth on 25 February 1967, he was so delighted that he kicked the ball over the stand and out of the Fratton Park ground. It was not retrieved and Knowles later received a bill, which he paid, for £7 10 shillings (£7.50) from Portsmouth, demanding the cost of a new one. For the record, Wolves won 3–2 and Knowles's goal was the winner!

**CENTENARY** Wolves celebrated their centenary in 1976–77 by winning the Second Division Championship and reaching the quarter-finals of the FA Cup.

**CENTRAL LEAGUE** The Central League originated in 1911 to serve primarily the clubs in the North and Midlands reserve teams. Wolves first played Central League football in 1921–22 after their reserve team had been members of the Birmingham and District League. They first won the championship in 1931–32 with 61 points, scoring 128 goals and conceding exactly half as many. Wolves won the title for a second time in 1950–51, scoring 110 goals of which centre-forward Ken Whitfield netted 29. The club again topped the hundred-goal mark the following season, scoring 101 times as they retained the Central League trophy. In 1952–53 Wolves completed a hat-trick of Central League Championship wins as they lost just seven of their matches. The club's fourth Central League title was won in 1957–58 when they scored 112 goals and conceded 64, including a 7–6 win over Manchester City. The following season Wolves won the title for a sixth and final time. They scored a remarkable 131 goals, won 32 of their 42 matches and lost just four games as they amassed 70 points. After 65 years of playing in the Central League, Wolves withdrew from the competition but re-entered in 1989–90 when it was renamed the Pontins League.

**CENTURIES** There are 11 instances of individual players who have scored 100 or more league goals for Wolves. Steve Bull is the greatest goalscorer with 246 strikes in his Molineux career (1986–1999). Other centurions are Billy Hartill (162); Johnny Hancocks (158); Jimmy Murray (155); John Richards (144); Peter Broadbent (127); Harry Wood (110); Roy Swinbourne (107); Dennis Westcott (105); Dennis Wilshaw (105) and Tom Phillipson (104). Phil Parkes holds the club record for the most consecutive league appearances – 127. Other players to have made over 100 consecutive appearances during their careers are Noel George (126); Cecil Shaw (120); Bobby Thomson (120); George Fleming (117); Derek Parkin (116); Jack Jones (109 and 102 in two spells) and Robbie Dennison (101).

**CHAMPIONSHIPS** Wolverhampton Wanderers are the only club to have won the championship of four divisions of the Football League plus the regional Third Division (North). The club won the Third Division (North) in 1923–24 when they finished the season one point ahead of runners-up Rochdale. In 1931–32, Wolves won the Second Division Championship. In what was virtually a two-horse race with Leeds United, the Wanderers lost only one in a run of 16 games after losing at Elland Road, producing some big wins, notably 7–1 at Port Vale and 7–0 over Manchester United at Molineux. Despite being held to a 1–1 draw when Leeds visited Molineux where Wilf Lowton missed a penalty, another seven-goal haul against Oldham Athletic helped the club keep their cool and pip their Yorkshire rivals by two points. During the 1950s, Wolves won the League Championship three times in the space of six seasons. The Molineux club first won the title in 1953–54 when they finished four points clear of rivals West Bromwich Albion whom Wolves beat 1–0 in both matches. Wolves won the title a second time in 1957–58. Despite a disappointing start to the season, they finished five points ahead of runners-up Preston North End after going 18 games without defeat. They seemed to be in line for a League and Cup double but lost 2–1 to Bolton Wanderers in one of the most exciting games ever witnessed at Burnden Park. Wolves retained the League Championship in 1958–59 despite losing four of their first ten matches. They finished six points ahead of Manchester United and scored a remarkable 110 goals. In 1976–77 Wolves won the Second Division Championship at the first attempt. After losing only one of their first eight matches, they strung together an unbeaten run of 12 games and after drawing 1–1 at home to Chelsea, their title rivals, they had to win at Bolton on the last day of the season. A goal from Kenny Hibbitt gave Wolves a 1–0 win and the title. Relegated to the Fourth Division in 1985–86, Wolves spent two seasons in the League's basement before winning the Championship in 1987–88, to become the first club to win all four divisions of the Football League. The club last won a divisional championship in 1988–89 when they won the Third Division title, finishing eight points clear of Sheffield United with a club record total of 92 points.

**CHAPMAN, SAMMY** Sammy Chapman was an attacking wing-half and a great favourite at Mansfield Town where he scored 41 goals in 168 games. After a spell with Portsmouth he became coach at Crewe Alexandra before joining Wolves as chief scout. Following the departure of Tommy Docherty, Chapman became the caretaker-manager until the arrival of Bill McGarry in September 1985. But McGarry left after just 61 days and Chapman was the surprise choice as manager of a club which had just been relegated to the Third Division for the first time since 1923. Sadly he was never really cut out to be a manager: Wolves were relegated again at the end of the 1985–86 campaign and in the summer he was relieved of his duties.

**CHARITY SHIELD** Wolverhampton Wanderers have appeared in five FA Charity Shield matches with the following results:

| Date | Opponents | Venue | Result |
|---|---|---|---|
| 19.10.1949 | Portsmouth | Highbury | 1–1 |
| 29.09.1954 | West Bromwich Albion | Molineux | 4–4 |
| 06.10.1958 | Bolton Wanderers | Burnden Park | 1–4 |
| 18.08.1959 | Nottingham Forest | Molineux | 3–1 |
| 13.08.1960 | Burnley | Turf Moor | 2–2 |

**CHATHAM, RAY** One of the club's most versatile players, Ray Chatham signed for Wolves as an amateur in the summer of 1942, though it was the 1945–46 season before he established himself as a first-team regular. During that campaign he was the club's top scorer with 14 goals in 30 games and scored both the club's goals in the 5–2 FA Cup defeat by Charlton Athletic. After making his Football League début in a 2–1 home defeat by Aston Villa on 11 September 1946, he was only chosen for a handful of games during the next five seasons. He then moved into a central defensive position and began to play on a more regular basis. He went on to play in 86 league and cup games for Wolves before leaving Molineux to play for Notts County. He soon settled in at Meadow Lane and over the next four seasons played in 128 league games before moving into non-league football with Margate.

**CHUNG, SAMMY** Sammy Chung, whose father was Chinese and his mother English, was a utility player who began his career as a part-time centre-forward with Headington United. He later joined Reading but didn't sign professional forms until he had completed his National Service. After a spell with Norwich City he joined Watford and played in 240 games for the Vicarage Road club, gaining his FA coaching badge whilst with that club. On leaving Watford and his role as player-coach, he joined Ipswich Town as coach under Bill McGarry, who had also been his boss at Vicarage Road. When McGarry became Wolves manager, Chung followed him to Molineux as trainer-coach before succeeding him in June 1976. His time wasn't a happy one, however, and with the fans calling for his head, he was sacked.

**CLAMP, EDDIE** One of the game's greatest characters in the 1950s and 1960s, Eddie Clamp was signed by Wolverhampton Wanderers midway through his newspaper round! Wolves sent him to play in their nursery side Wath Wanderers and in April 1952 he turned professional. Affectionately nicknamed 'Chopper', he made his first-team début for Wolves in a 1–0 defeat against Manchester United at Old Trafford on 6 March 1954. Whilst with Wolves, he won four full caps for England when the half-back line read Clamp-Wright-Slater. Earlier in his career he had played four times for England Schoolboys and represented the Football League on four occasions. Clamp also won two League Championship medals in 1958 and 1959 and an FA Cup winners' medal in 1960 as Blackburn Rovers were beaten 3–0. He had scored 25 goals in 241 games for Wolves when, in November 1961, he was transferred to Arsenal for £30,000. The Gunners had hoped his experience would guide the younger players within their squad. However, after only ten months and 22 league appearances, he was transferred to Stoke City for £15,000. In his first season at the Victoria Ground, he helped the Potters win the Second Division Championship and was sent off in a home game against Burnley after a fracas with England winger John Connelly. After Stoke he played for Peterborough United, Worcester City and Lower Gornal before leaving the game in 1969 to concentrate on his own business interests.

**CLARKE, WAYNE** Much travelled striker Wayne Clarke began his career with Wolverhampton Wanderers. A member of a famous

*Wayne Clarke*

footballing family, four of his brothers having played league football, he made his début for the Molineux club as a substitute in a 2–1 win at Ipswich Town on the last day of the 1977–78 season. It took him a few seasons to establish himself in the Wolves side and it wasn't until 1982–83, when the club won promotion to the First Division, that he showed his prowess as a goalscorer when he netted 12 times in 39 games. He had scored 33 goals in 170 games for Wolves when he joined Birmingham City in the summer of 1984. He continued to find the net for the Blues and scored 43 goals in 105 games including 18 in the first two-thirds of the 1986–87 campaign, which prompted Everton to pay £300,000 for him in March 1987. He soon settled at Goodison and helped the club win the League Championship for the second time in three years as well as scoring the only goal in the 1987 Charity Shield win over Coventry City. He later played for Manchester City and Walsall before returning to Wolves on loan where he made one more appearance. He ended his career with Shrewsbury, whom he helped win the Third Division Championship in 1993–94.

**CLAYTON, GORDON** Sunderland-born centre-forward Gordon Clayton joined Wolves from Shotton Colliery in October 1932. A former policeman, he had to wait until April 1934 before making his début when he returned to the north-east, only to be on the losing side – Wolves lost 5–1 to Newcastle United. Over the next four seasons, Clayton appeared in only a handful of matches before teaming up with Tom Galley in 1936–37. That season, Wolves finished fifth in Division One and reached the sixth round of the FA Cup where they lost after two replays to Clayton's home-town club. It was undoubtedly Clayton's best season with the Molineux club, scoring 29 goals in 39 games including four in a 7–2 win over Everton and a hat-trick in a 5–2 defeat of Grimsby Town. He went on to score 39 goals in only 55 appearances before joining Aston Villa. He helped Villa win the Second Division Championship before moving to Burnley. He later 'guested' for Swansea Town during the Second World War before hanging up his boots.

**CLEAN SHEETS** This is the colloquial expression used to describe a goalkeeper's performance when he does not concede a goal. In 1923–24, Noel George kept 23 clean sheets in 42 games as Wolves ended the season as champions of the Third Division (North).

**CLERGYMEN** The only occasion in Football League history of two clergymen playing in the same side occurred in the 1912–13 season when Wolverhampton Wanderers fielded the Reverend Kenneth Hunt as half-back and the Reverend Bill Jordan as a forward.

**COLLINS, TED** Ted Collins played his early football with Brownhills Athletic before signing for Wolves in the summer of 1907. He made his début in a 2–1 home defeat by West Bromwich Albion on the opening day of the 1907–08 season. At the end of that campaign, Collins won an FA Cup winners' medal after Wolves had beaten Newcastle United in the final. Forming an outstanding full-back partnership with Jack Jones, Collins went on to appear in 307 games for the club before leaving Molineux in 1915 to join Newport County. Unfortunately the outbreak of the First World War meant that he never played for the Welsh club. In 1915–16 he 'guested' for Walsall and in a match against Cannock, when pressed into service as an emergency centre-forward, he scored five goals after not finding the net once during his Wolves days.

**COLOURS** Wolves played for the first time in their famous gold and black jerseys at the start of the 1891–92 season. Earlier they wore an assortment of strips that included red and white stripes, blue and black, pink and white and, on a few occasions, even squares! During the 1923–24 season, Wolves wore a new away strip which consisted of the gold-coloured shirts with a large black 'V' which stretched from the shoulders to the waist. When Major Frank Buckley became Wolves' manager in 1927 he immediately asked for a new club strip – black and gold vertical striped shirts, black shorts, black socks – similar to the one worn by the players either side of the First World War. Though they once had a spell playing in all gold, the club's present colours are gold shirts, black shorts and gold stockings, with change colours of white shirts and teal shorts.

**CONSECUTIVE HOME GAMES** Wolverhampton Wanderers have played an extraordinary, intense sequence of five home games in succession on three occasions. The first was between 22 December 1894 and 12 January 1895 with the following results:

| | | | |
|---|---|---|---|
| 22 December 1894 | Aston Villa | Lost | 0–4 |
| 26 December 1894 | Burnley | Won | 1–0 |

| 27 December 1894 | | West Brom Albion | Won | 3–1 |
| 5 January | 1895 | Everton | Won | 1–0 |
| 12 January | 1895 | Sunderland | Lost | 1–4 |

The second occasion was at the end of the 1898–99 season with the following results:

| 1 April 1899 | Stoke | Won | 3–2 |
| 3 April 1899 | Aston Villa | Won | 4–0 |
| 4 April 1899 | Bolton Wanderers | Won | 1–0 |
| 15 April 1899 | Burnley | Won | 4–0 |
| 29 April 1899 | Everton | Lost | 1–2 |

The last occasion when Wolves played five home games in succession was between 4 and 25 March 1978.

| 4 March 1978 | Norwich City | Drew | 3–3 |
| 11 March 1978 | West Ham United | Won | 2–1 |
| 14 March 1978 | West Brom Albion | Drew | 1–1 |
| 18 March 1978 | Manchester City | Drew | 1–1 |
| 25 March 1978 | Liverpool | Lost | 1–3 |

**CONSECUTIVE SCORING – LONGEST SEQUENCE** Tom Phillipson holds the club record for consecutive scoring when he was on target in 13 consecutive league games during the 1926–27 season. He netted a hat-trick in the 9–1 home win over Barnsley on 5 November 1926 and ended the sequence with the opening goal in a 2–2 draw at Notts County on 9 February 1927. During the sequence the Ryton-on-Tyne-born forward scored 22 goals including 5 in a 7–2 home win over Bradford City.

**COOK, PAUL** Liverpool-born Paul Cook began his career with Marine before turning professional with Wigan Athletic in the summer of 1984. After scoring 14 goals in 93 League and Cup games, he was transferred to Norwich City for £73,000 in June 1988. Unable to win a regular first-team place with the Canaries he moved to Molineux in November 1989, joining Wolves for a fee of £250,000. He made his début in a goalless draw at Leicester City and impressed over the next couple of seasons with his probing passes and powerful long-range shots. After a series of niggling injuries and a loss of form, Cook, who had scored 21 goals in 214 games, joined Coventry City for £600,000. His form for the Sky Blues was patchy and after spending much of 1995–96 on the sidelines, he left Highfield Road to join Tranmere Rovers. At Prenton Park he was called upon to play in a variety of positions but he always proved dependable and had made 69 appearances before signing for Stockport County for a club-record fee of £250,000. Despite fracturing his skull in a fall at home, he made an unexpected comeback towards the end of the 1997–98 season.

**CRAWFORD, RAY** Ray Crawford began his league career with his home-town club Portsmouth but after netting 12 goals in 22 games for the Fratton Park club he joined Ipswich in September 1958. He played his first game for Town the following month, scoring both goals in a 4–2 defeat at Swansea. That season he was the club's top scorer with 25 goals in 30 League games including a hat-trick at Portman Road in the return game against Swansea and another in a 5–3 win over Brighton and Hove Albion. Developing a fine understanding with Ted Phillips, he scored 40 of the club's 100 League goals when they won the Second Division Championship in 1960–61. He scored three hat-tricks against Brighton (Away 4–2), Leeds United (Away 5–2) and Leyton Orient (Home 6–2). The following season he scored 33 goals in 41 games as Ipswich won the League Championship and he became the first player from the Portman Road club to gain an England cap whilst on Town's books. He had another outstanding season in 1962–63, playing in every match and scoring 25 goals. It was also the club's first experience of European football and when they beat the Maltese champions Floriana 10–0 at home, Crawford scored five of the goals to establish a scoring record for any British player in any European competition. He also netted a hat-trick for the Football League against the Irish League at Carrow Road. In September 1963, Crawford was, surprisingly, allowed to leave Portman Road and join Wolverhampton Wanderers. He made his début in a disastrous 6–0 defeat at Liverpool but then proceeded to score 26 goals in 34 games to become the club's top scorer. Included in that total was a hat-trick in the final game of the season at Bolton as Wolves beat the Trotters 4–0 to send the Lancashire club into the Second Division. Despite being hampered by injury in 1964–65, he continued to find the back of the net but after scoring 41 goals in 61 League and Cup games, he left Molineux to join West Bromwich Albion. He never settled at The Hawthorns and returned to Ipswich where he took his club record to 228 goals in 354 games before joining Charlton Athletic. After a spell playing non-League football for Kettering Town he joined Colchester United and, scoring a hat-trick in a 3–0 FA Cup first-round win over Ringmer, became the first player to score hat-tricks in the Football League, League Cup, FA Cup and European Cup.

**CROOK, BILLY** A stockily built wing-half, Billy Crook joined Wolves in 1940 and appeared in 121 games during the Second World War before making his League début in a 2–0 defeat at Blackpool in September 1946. That season, Crook missed just three games as the Wanderers finished third in Division One. He scored his first goal for the club in a 6–1 home win over Huddersfield Town. He won an FA Cup winners' medal in 1949 as Wolves beat Leicester City 3–1 and played in 34 games in 1949–50 when the Molineux club finished runners-up to Portsmouth in the First Division. He went on to appear in 221 League and Cup games before joining Walsall. After leaving Fellows Park he went into non-League football and retired in 1960.

**CROWD TROUBLE** However unwelcome, crowd disturbances at major football are far from a modern phenomenon. Though behaviour at Molineux in recent years has usually been of a high standard, there were occasions in the club's early years when incidents of crowd trouble occurred. On 18 October 1919, Wolves, who were entertaining Bury, were trailing 1–0 when the referee awarded the visitors a penalty. A number of Wolves supporters on the Molineux Street side of the ground ran on to the pitch and surrounded the referee, who decided to make a run for the changing-rooms. Unfortunately he fell to his knees as he crossed the halfway line and though players from both sides, along with the police who had emerged from the stands, tried to assist the referee, it was to no avail. Finally, a rather battered and bruised referee was led to safety but the damage had been done: Molineux was closed for two home matches. When Wolves entertained Chelsea on 7 November 1936, there was crowd trouble at the end of the game, which the visitors won 2–1. Nearly 2,000 Wolves supporters ran on to the pitch and almost uprooted the goalposts. On this occasion, however, the club escaped with just a severe reprimand from the FA. One of the most recent incidents of crowd trouble occurred on 25 May 1987 when Wolves played Aldershot in a second-leg tie in the play-offs. Aldershot won 1–0 (3–0 on aggregate) and condemned the Molineux club to another season of Fourth Division football. At the end of the match several policemen were injured and there were numerous arrests.

**CULLIS, STAN** One of the few men to achieve success both as a player and a manager, Stan Cullis joined Wolves from Ellesmere Port Wednesday in February 1934. Twelve months later he made his League début for the Molineux club in a 3–2 home defeat by Huddersfield Town. He was appointed captain of the Wolves first team before he was 20 and in later years captained his country. With England, he won 12 full caps plus a further 20 in wartime internationals when he formed a brilliant half-back line with Cliff Britton and Joe Mercer. He had appeared for Wolves in the last pre-war FA Cup final when the Molineux club lost 4–1 to Portsmouth at Wembley and, though he lost seven seasons' football due to the Second World War, he was a first team regular in 1946–47 when League football resumed. He retired from playing at the end of that season, having appeared in 171 League and Cup games for the club. He then became assistant to Ted Vizard at Molineux before being appointed manager in June 1948. Cullis signed and developed a number of outstanding footballers and pioneered floodlit friendlies. Under his guidance, Wolves won three League titles in 1953–54, 1957–58 and 1958–59. They also lifted the FA Cup twice in 1949 and 1960, the FA Charity Shield and the FA Youth Cup, and they entered European competition in the late 1950s. Sadly, after 1961, things began to go wrong and attendances declined as Wolves found themselves near the foot of the First Division. Cullis was sacked in September 1964 – his dismissal leading to bitter recriminations from Wolves fans and media alike. He then had a year out of the game before taking charge of Birmingham City. He led the Blues to the semi-finals of both the FA and League Cups but fans were hoping he would lead their club back into the top flight. It wasn't to be, however, and in March 1970 he parted company with the St Andrew's club.

*Stan Cullis*

*Keith Curle*

**CURLE, KEITH** Keith Curle began his career as an associated
schoolboy with Bristol City but then switched his allegiance to

Bristol Rovers, first as an apprentice and then as a professional. He made his Football League début for the Pirates in a 2–2 draw at home to Chester City in August 1981 and scored the equaliser for Rovers. After failing to command a regular place, he was transferred to Torquay United but four months later left to sign  for Bristol City. After three seasons with the Ashton Gate club, in which he was converted from midfield to central defence, he moved to Reading. His outstanding displays in the heart of the Royals' defence prompted Wimbledon to sign him. Forming a formidable defensive partnership with Eric Young, he captained the 'Dons' with distinction. However, it was still a great surprise when Peter Reid signed him for Manchester City for a fee of £2.5 million in the summer of 1991. Curle eventually won full England honours when he came on as a substitute against the CIS in Mexico in April 1992, following it with his full début in Hungary two weeks later. He captained the Maine Road club during the first Premier League season of 1992–93 and made 204 appearances before leaving to join Wolves for £650,000 in August 1996. Signed to replace Adrian Williams, who had been injured before he could make his début, he too required surgery after a substitute appearance at Oxford in September 1996 and didn't make his full début until January 1997 in a 2–0 home win over West Bromwich Albion. Outstanding in the play-offs, Curle had another good season in 1997–98 where his organisational skills were very much in evidence.

**CURRAN, HUGH** Although he was born in Glasgow, Hugh Curran grew up in Ireland and played part-time for Shamrock Rovers before the family returned to live in Scotland. After trials with Third Lanark and Morton, Curran joined Millwall and in his first full season at The Den, 1964–65, top-scored with 18 League goals. He had scored 26 goals in 57 games when Norwich City paid £12,000 to take him to Carrow Road in January 1966. After being hampered by injuries in his first two seasons with the Canaries, he was the club's only ever-present in 1967–68 when he top-scored with 16 goals including a hat-trick in a 4–2 win over Birmingham City. The following season he was still the club's top scorer with 22 goals in 31 League and Cup games before being transferred to Wolverhampton Wanderers for £60,000 in January 1969. The following month Curran played his first game for the Molineux club in a 1–1 home draw against Burnley and, in 1969–70, he was Wolves' top scorer

*Hugh Curran*

with 20 goals in 38 League games. His first hat-trick for the club came the following season in a 4–0 home win over Nottingham Forest but in September 1972, after scoring 47 goals in 98 games, he left to join Oxford United. Whilst at Molineux, he won five full caps for Scotland and helped the club to the final of the UEFA Cup. After scoring 26 goals in 70 League games for Oxford United he joined Bolton Wanderers where he top-scored in his only full season at Burnden Park. He later had a second spell with Oxford United where he took his tally of League goals to 37 in 105 games before retiring through injury in March 1979.

# D

**DALEY, STEVE** An England Youth international, Steve Daley joined Wolves as an apprentice and signed as a professional in 1971. It took him a number of seasons to establish a regular first-team place after making his début as a substitute in a 4–2 win over Nottingham Forest in September 1971. In fact, when he did win a regular spot, Wolves were slipping out of the top flight in 1976 but he was an ever-present the following season and the Molineux club made a swift return to the First Division. He scored 13 goals, easily the best of his career. In the summer of 1978, Daley was selected for the England 'B' tour of Australia and won his first cap at that level in a 1–1 draw against Malaysia. After another season at Molineux, Daley, who had scored 43 goals in 244 games, joined Manchester City for a British record transfer fee of £1,437,500. Having spent a little over a year at Maine Road, he crossed the Atlantic to play for Seattle Sounders in the NASL. He later returned to England to play for Burnley, scoring a hat-trick for the Clarets in a 3–2 win over Port Vale. After another spell in America, he ended his league career with Walsall.

**DANIEL, PETER** Peter Daniel joined his home-town club Hull City and after making his first team début in 1974, immediately became a regular on the side. Impressing at right- or left-back, he won the first of seven England Under-21 caps against Scotland at Bramall Lane in April 1977. After City were relegated to the Third Division in 1978, he joined Wolverhampton Wanderers for £150,000. He had been converted to a midfield player by this time but his first season at Molineux ended in disappointment as Wolves were beaten by Arsenal in an FA Cup semi-final at Villa Park. In 1980 he won a League Cup winners' medal as Wolves beat Nottingham Forest in the final. Sadly, a broken leg sustained in a match against Aston Villa

*Steve Daley*

in February 1981 kept him out of another run to the FA Cup semi-final where Wolves were beaten by Spurs in a replay at Highbury. Relegation in 1982 was followed by instant promotion in 1983 but after a spell with NASL side, Minnesota Kicks, Daniel, who had scored 16 goals in 194 games, left Wolves for Sunderland. In his first season at Roker Park he endured mixed emotions as the Wearsiders reached the League Cup final at Wembley but also lost their First Division status. He then joined Lincoln City, later being appointed player-manager, but after the Sincil Bank club became the first team to be automatically relegated to the Vauxhall Conference, he left and joined Burnley. In May 1988 he played against Wolves in the Sherpa Van Trophy final at Wembley but retired six months later, after having played in 400 league games for his five clubs.

**DAVIES, FRED** Liverpool-born goalkeeper Fred Davies began his career with Llandudno Town before signing for Wolverhampton Wanderers in April 1957. Initially he was unable to break into the first team at Molineux and he spent four seasons in the club's Central League side before being given his chance. His League début came on 3 February 1962 as Wolves beat Tottenham Hotspur 3–1 in front of a Molineux crowd of 45,687. He went on to appear in 173 League and Cup games for Wolves, helping them win promotion to the First Division in 1966–67, but in January 1968 he left to join Cardiff City for a fee of £10,000. He ended his first season at Ninian Park with a Welsh Cup winners' medal and in 1968–69 was an ever-present as the club came close to winning promotion to the top flight. After appearing in 128 games for the Bluebirds, he left to join Bournemouth. He starred in the south-coast club's Fourth Division promotion-winning side of 1970–71 and went on to play in 134 League games for the Cherries before coaching at a number of clubs.

**DEACON, JIM** Glasgow-born forward Jim Deacon began his career with Third Division Darlington but after two seasons with the Quakers he moved south to join Wolverhampton Wanderers in the summer of 1929. He scored on his Wolves' début in a 2–2 draw at Bradford City after which he was a first-team regular for the next four seasons. In 1931–32 his 13 goals helped Wolves win the Second Division Championship, whilst his best season in terms of League goals scored was 1932–33 as the club sought to consolidate themselves in the top flight. One of the most skilful inside-forwards ever to appear for the club, he was a big favourite with both players and supporters. He went on to score 55 goals in 158 League and Cup games before leaving Molineux in October 1934 to join Southend United. In the summer of 1939 he returned to the north-east to join Hartlepool United but after just three League appearances, the League was suspended on the outbreak of the Second World War and Jim Deacon, whose brother Richard also played for Wolves, found his career was over.

**DEELEY, NORMAN** Wednesbury-born winger Norman Deeley was the smallest player ever to represent England Schoolboys, being just 4ft 4ins tall in 1947–48. His size did not deter Wolves and they signed him as an amateur before he turned professional in December 1950. He played his first game for the club at right-half as Wolves beat Arsenal 2–1 at Molineux. After two years, National Service, Deeley was switched to the right-wing and scored his first goal for the club in the FA Charity Shield against West Bromwich Albion in September 1954. However, it wasn't until the 1957–58 season that Deeley established himself as a regular first-team member, after which he missed very few games. He won League Championship medals in 1957–58 and 1958–59 when he scored 23 and 17 league goals respectively. His total in 1958–59 included his first hat-trick for the club in a 7–0 home win over Portsmouth. On 16 September 1959, Deeley scored four goals in the 9–0 demolition of Fulham in front of 41,692 fans at Molineux. He also scored two of Wolves' goals in the 3–0 FA Cup final win over Blackburn Rovers in 1960 but in February 1962, Deeley, who had won two full caps for England, left to join Leyton Orient after scoring 75 goals in 237 games. On leaving Brisbane Road he played non-league football for Worcester City, Bromsgrove Rovers and Darlaston before hanging up his boots.

**DEFEATS – FEWEST** During the 1923–24 season, Wolverhampton Wanderers made their way through the 42-match programme and suffered only three defeats and won the Third Division (North) Championship. In more recent years, the club lost just six of their 46 matches in 1988–89 as they once again won the Third Division title.

**DEFEATS – MOST** A total of 25 defeats suffered during each of the seasons 1964–65, 1983–84, 1984–85 and 1985–86 are the worst in the club's history. Not surprisingly the club were relegated on each occasion.

**DEFEATS – WORST** Wolverhampton Wanderer's record defeat came on 15 October 1892 when they travelled to Newton Heath and were beaten 10–1. The club's worst home defeat was 8–0 by West Bromwich Albion on 27 December 1893.

**DEFENSIVE RECORDS** Wolverhampton Wanderers' best defensive record was established in 1923–24 when the club won the Third Division (North) Championship. They conceded just 27 goals in that campaign of 42 matches, losing on just three occasions. The club's worst defensive record was in 1905–06 when they let in 99 goals to finish bottom of the First Division.

**DENNISON, ROBBIE** Northern Ireland international winger Robbie Dennison joined West Bromwich Albion from Irish League club Glenavon for £40,000 in September 1985. His opportunities at The Hawthorns were limited and in March 1987 Graham Turner brought him to Molineux for a cut-price fee of £20,000. Playing wide on the left, he made his début in a 4–0 home win over Swansea City and won a regular place in the Wolves side with immediate effect. He helped Wolves win the Fourth and Third Division Championships in consecutive seasons and in 1988 scored in the 2–0 win over Burnley in the final of the Sherpa Van Trophy. He was the only ever-present in 1989–90 and, during this spell, appeared in 101 consecutive League games. He missed very few games for the club until the mid-1990s when he went on loan to Swansea City. An excellent crosser of the ball, he returned to Molineux where he continued to set up chances for his colleagues. At the end of the 1996–97 season he was released after scoring 50 goals in 353 first-team games.

**DERBIES** Wolverhampton Wanderers and West Bromwich Albion have met on many occasions in what has become known as the 'Black Country Derby'. The two rivals first met in the Birmingham Cup in 1882 at Four Acres when Albion won 4–2. They also eliminated the Wanderers from the semi-final of the Birmingham Cup in 1883–84 and it wasn't until 1885, that Wolves overcame their local rivals 2–0 in a friendly and thereby won for the first time. The clubs were first drawn together in the FA Cup in 1885–86 when Albion won 3–1 at Stoney Lane. Their first league meeting was on 15 December 1888 at the Wolverhampton club's Dudley Road ground. Hunter and Brodie scored for Wolves in a 2–1 win and they then completed the double with a 3–1 success at Stoney Lane. By the start of the following season, Wolves had moved to Molineux and the first meeting at the ground ended all square at 1–1. In 1893 the Baggies gained their biggest ever win against the Wanderers when they won 8–0 at Molineux. Wolves gained some revenge with 6–1 and 5–1 victories in 1896 and 1898. Up until 1903 all the meetings between the two clubs had been in the First Division but 1906 found both teams relegated. Albion won promotion in 1909–10 as Second Division champions after both clubs had each won six of their 12 meetings in the Division. It was a further 17 years before the clubs met again and once more it was in the Second Division. After four seasons, Albion were promoted to the First Division but it was 1931–32 before the Molineux club won back their top flight status. During the next six seasons, the Baggies won five and drew three of the twelve meetings until they were relegated in 1937–38, despite the fact that Wolves, under Major Frank Buckley, were one of the country's leading sides. Wolves' only success in ten FA Cup ties between the clubs came in 1948–49 when a goal by Jimmy Mullen helped them on their way to winning the FA Cup that season. Following West Brom's promotion in 1948–49, the two clubs met for the first time in post-war football and the highest attendances for the 'Black Country Derby' were set at both grounds during the season. On 15 October 1949, a crowd of 56,661 packed into Molineux to watch Jesse Pye score for Wolves in a 1–1 draw. The return game at The Hawthorns also finished 1–1 with Johnny Hancocks netting for Wolves, watched by 60,945 people. There then followed an uninterrupted spell of 16 seasons of First Division meetings between the clubs with Wolves only losing twice. The Molineux club's best win during this period was a 7–0 triumph in 1962–63 with both Terry Wharton and Alan Hinton scoring hat-tricks. Wolves were relegated to the Second Division in 1965 but after two seasons the local derby was resumed until 1973 when the Baggies lost their top-flight status. The derby was restored again in 1977–78 when Wolves, who had been relegated in 1975–76 ,won the Second Division Championship at their first attempt. Remarkably, after a series of high-scoring encounters, six of the two clubs' next meetings ended in draws, producing just 16 goals. Over the past few seasons Albion have had the better of things, though in 1996–97,Wolves did complete the 'double' over their rivals, and in a 4–2 win at The Hawthorns, Iwan Roberts netted a hat-trick. The record for most appearances made in this fixture by a Wolves player is 26, held by Peter Broadbent, whilst Johnny Hancocks and Jim Murray are the leading scorers with nine goals apiece. Wolverhampton Wanderers' record against West Bromwich Albion up until the end of the 1997–98 season is as follows:

|                 | P   | W  | D  | L  | F   | A   |
|-----------------|-----|----|----|----|-----|-----|
| Football League | 130 | 48 | 34 | 48 | 212 | 207 |
| FA Cup          | 10  | 1  | 2  | 7  | 7   | 16  |
| Total           | 140 | 49 | 36 | 55 | 219 | 223 |

**DISMISSALS** A number of players have been sent off whilst playing for Wolves. When the club won the Second Division Championship in 1931–32 they lost both games to Stoke and, in the second of these meetings, Billy Barraclough received his marching orders. Charlie Phillips was Wolves captain when he was dismissed in the match against Bolton Wanderers in December 1935, and a month later he was sold to Aston Villa. Dave Woodfield became the first Wolves player to be sent off at Molineux for some 30 years when he was dismissed in the match against Manchester City in August 1965. Goalkeeper Phil Parkes was sent off in the local derby against West Bromwich Albion in August 1967 after saving a Tony Brown penalty! David Wagstaffe who was once sent off for Wolves against Blackburn Rovers, became the first League player to be shown a red card when playing for Blackburn Rovers after leaving Molineux. During the 1969–70 season, Derek Dougan was sent off twice. After being dismissed in the 3–2 win against Sheffield Wednesday at Hillsborough for which he received a suspended 14-day ban, he was sent off again two months later in the 3–2 win over Everton. He then received a six-week ban which was added to his earlier suspended sentence!

**DOCHERTY, TOMMY** Glasgow-born Tommy Docherty had worked his way up through Celtic's junior ranks and served with the Highland Light Infantry for two years in Palestine before joining Preston North End in November 1949 for £4,000. A fearless winghalf, he was capable of dispossessing the best of opponents and instantly turning defence into attack with the drive of an aggressive ball player. A terror in the tackle, 'The Doc' had the cure for most inside-forwards – they were never keen on a second visit! He won the first of 25 Scottish caps against Wales in 1952 but after playing in 324 out of a possible 356 games, and missing 21 through injury and 7 through international calls, he moved to Arsenal for £28,000 in August 1958. Tragically ironic for Docherty was his misfortune in breaking a leg when playing for the Gunners against Preston. He packed away his boots to become senior coach to Chelsea before being appointed caretaker-manager in September 1961. Four months later his appointment was confirmed on a permanent basis and in 1967 he took the young Chelsea side to the FA Cup final where they lost 2–1 to Spurs. One of the game's most controversial characters, he was an outspoken and much-travelled manager. He left Chelsea in 1967 and after a year in charge of Rotherham United he took on the challenge of Queen's Park Rangers. He left, however, within a month. He joined Aston Villa but, following one of the worst seasons in the club's history, he was sacked in January 1970. After a spell with Porto he was appointed Scotland's team manager, giving them an immediate boost before succeeding Frank O'Farrell at Manchester United. In four and a half seasons at Old Trafford he assembled an exciting side and led them to success in the FA Cup final of 1977. He later managed Derby County, Queen's Park Rangers (again!) and, after a spell in Australia, Preston North End. In June 1984 he was appointed manager of Wolverhampton Wanderers but the club finished bottom of the Second Division in 1984–85 and, though Docherty tried his best to save them, a run of 21 games without a win meant the situation could not be saved and in July 1985 he was sacked.

**DODD, ALAN** After beginning his career with Stoke City, Alan Dodd developed into one of the best central defenders in the club's post-war history. He emerged in the 1970s though initially he had to compete with Stoke's formidable central pairing of Denis Smith and Alan Bloor. Dodd was skilful in the air and on the ground was the perfect example of consistency, making 102 consecutive league appearances between January 1976 and April 1978. However, his concentration seemed to lapse on the odd occasion and this probably accounted for his failure to win full England honours when he seemed to be on the verge of adding to his six Under-23 caps. When Alan Durban became manager, he was less impressed by 'Doddy' and he was moved into midfield or played at full-back. He was eventually sold to Wolverhampton Wanderers for £40,000 in November 1982 and after making his début in a 4–3 win at Crystal

Palace, he played in the remaining 27 games of the season as the Molineux club won promotion to the First Division. He had appeared in 99 games for Wolves when in January 1985 he returned to the Victoria Ground, but he had lost his pace and was cruelly exposed by a number of top flight players as the club were relegated. He later had spells at Elfsborg, GAIS Gothenburg, Port Vale, Cork City, Landskrona, Bols, Rocester, Goldenhill Wanderers and Rocester again as player-coach.

**DORSETT, DICKY** Nicknamed the 'Brownhills Bomber', Dicky Dorsett began his league career with Wolverhampton Wanderers and made his début in a 4–1 defeat at Charlton Athletic on 26 March 1938. Three weeks later he scored four goals when Wolves demolished Leicester City 10–1, a feat he repeated on 22 February 1939 as Everton were beaten 7–0 in front of a Molineux crowd of 39,734. At the end of that season, he scored Wolves' goal in their 4–1 defeat by Portsmouth in the 1939 FA Cup final. During the war he served in the RAF and 'guested' for Liverpool, Grimsby Town, Brentford, Queen's Park Rangers and Southampton. He was a member of the Wolves side that beat Sunderland in the 1942 Wartime League Cup final but left Molineux in 1946 to join Aston Villa. During the war, he scored 42 goals in 61 games including four in a 5–5 draw against Walsall and 35 goals in 52 League and Cup games. On his arrival at Villa Park, Dorsett switched from forward to wing-half or left-back, though he did manage to score 36 goals in 271 games for the Villans. After retiring from the playing side of the game at the end of the 1952–53 season, he stayed at Villa Park to coach the club's youth team. In the summer of 1957 he was appointed Liverpool's assistant-trainer but five years later returned to the Midlands to take over the running of a junior side.

**DOUGAN, DEREK** Born in Belfast, Derek Dougan started his career as a centre-half and was capped for Ireland at schoolboy level before joining Distillery where he won youth and amateur recognition for his country. Switching to centre-forward, he joined Portsmouth in the summer of 1957 but after just 33 games for the Fratton Park club, he left to play for First Division Blackburn Rovers. At Ewood Park he scored 25 goals in 59 league games and was in the Blackburn side that lost the 1960 FA Cup final to Wolverhampton Wanderers. Following Gerry Hitchens' departure to Inter Milan, Aston Villa

*Derek Dougan*

paid £15,000 to bring the popular Irishman to Villa Park. After making his début in the opening game of the 1961–62 season he suffered various injuries but nonetheless scored 12 goals in 27 appearances during that campaign. The following season he scored his only hat-trick for the club in a 6–1 FA Cup win over Peterborough United. He moved to 'The Posh' in the summer of 1963 before having a spell with Leicester City where he scored 35 goals in 68 league games. In March 1967 he joined Wolves and in just over eight seasons at Molineux he scored 123 goals in 323 games. Chairman of the PFA and the winner of 43 caps for Northern Ireland, he helped Wolves win promotion to the First Division at the end of his first season with the club, scoring nine goals in 11 games including a hat-trick in a 4–0 home win over Hull City. He was Wolves' top scorer in 1967–68 with 17 goals including a hat-trick in the 6–1 defeat of Nottingham Forest. He topped the scoring charts again the following season and in 1971–72 when he helped Wolves reach the final of the UEFA Cup. He won a League Cup winners' medal in 1974. After leaving the first-class game in 1975, he managed Kettering Town, later returning to Molineux as chairman and chief executive, a position he held only briefly before circumstances forced him out of office.

**DOWNING, KEITH** Nicknamed 'Psycho' by the Molineux faithful, following his aggressive displays in the club's midfield, he began his career with Mile Oak Rovers before joining Notts County. After three years with the Meadow Lane club, in which he made just 23 League appearances, he joined Wolves in the summer of 1987. He made his début as a substitute in the opening match of the 1987–88 season, a 2–2 draw at Scarborough. He went on to appear in 34 league games that season as Wolves won the Fourth Division Championship and was a member of the side that won the Sherpa Van Trophy. In 1988–89 he helped the club win the Third Division Championship and continued to be an important member of the side for the next few seasons. Sadly a series of injuries marred his last few months with the club and in the summer of 1993, after appearing in 228 games for Wolves, he left to join Birmingham City. Having played only two games for the Blues he suffered a serious leg injury and eventually moved to Stoke City where, after playing in 24 games, he was freed during the summer of 1995. After a short spell with Cardiff City, he helped Hereford United reach the play-offs. However, throughout his stay at Edgar Street he suffered from injuries and, after appearing in 55 games, he was forced to retire with a chronic back ailment.

**DRAWS** Wolverhampton Wanderers played their greatest number of drawn League matches in a single season in 1990–91 when 19 of their matches ended all square, and their fewest drawn League matches in seasons 1888–89, 1891–92, 1892–93, 1904–05 and 1964–65 when only four of their matches were drawn. The club's highest scoring draw is 4–4, a scoreline achieved in the following six League games – Accrington (Away 1888–89), Bradford Park Avenue (Home 1929–30), Derby County (Away 1932–33), Middlesbrough (Away 1948–49), Arsenal (Away 1959–60) and Newcastle United (Away 1960–61).

**DUNN, JIMMY** The son of the former Everton and Scotland international of the same name, he joined Wolves as an amateur in 1941 and though he had some success with the Molineux club during the war years, he made only three appearances when peacetime football resumed in 1946–47. It was midway through the following season when he won a regular place in the club's starting line-up and in 1949 he collected an FA Cup winners' medal after an outstanding season which had seen him score eight goals in 35 games. After just a handful of games in 1949–50 he was troubled by a serious back injury that forced him to miss the rest of the campaign. He fought his way back to full fitness and on 13 October 1951 scored his first hat-trick for the club in a 7–1 win at Huddersfield Town. He had scored 39 goals in 140 games when he left Molineux to join Derby County. After only a few weeks at the Baseball Ground, Dunn was forced to undergo a cartilage operation and, though he went on to score 21 goals in 58 games, he was transferred to Worcester City of the Southern League. He later played for Runcorn before becoming a coach at West Bromwich Albion.

# E

**EARLY GROUNDS** After their formation in 1877, the club's first ground was at Windmill Field on Goldthorn Road before moving two years later to John Harper's Field on Lower Villiers Street. In 1881, after the club had adopted the name Wolverhampton Wanderers, they moved to a field on Dudley Road opposite the Fighting Cock pub. Also behind this piece of land was the Blakenhall Wanderers cricket ground where the club later played a number of games. The ground at Dudley Road was never really developed and in 1889, at the end of their first season in the Football League – a campaign in which they also reached the FA Cup final – they left to play at the Molineux Grounds.

**EDMONDS, GEORGE** A centre-forward in the old-fashioned mode, George Edmonds joined Watford as a professional in 1912 and in 1914–15 helped them win the Southern League Championship. Whilst with Watford, he played for England in a Victory International but in June 1920 he moved to Wolverhampton Wanderers for a fee of £1,500. He made his début in a 2–0 defeat at Fulham on the opening day of the 1920–21 season and went on to end the campaign as the club's leading scorer with 15 league and cup goals as the Molineux side reached the FA Cup final where they lost 1–0 to Spurs. Forming a fine striking partnership with Stan Fazackerly, he was the club's leading scorer in each of his three full seasons with the club. His only hat-trick came on 2 April 1923 when he scored all of the club's goals in a 3–0 home win over Port Vale. Sadly, at the end of that season Wolves were relegated to the Third Division (North) and Edmonds became unsettled and wanted to leave. In September 1923, after scoring 42 goals in 126 first-team games, he moved to Fulham but was unable to force his way into the Cottagers' first team and within 12 months had left to play non-League football.

**EMBLEN, NEIL** Millwall paid non-League Sittingbourne £175,000 for the services of Neil Emblen in November 1993 but after just 12 League games for the Lions he joined Wolves, who paid the London club £600,000 in the summer of 1994. A most versatile player, he made his début in the opening game of the 1994–95 season as Wolves beat Reading at Molineux 1–0. Since then, his time at Molineux has been blighted by injuries and suspension but, despite a torn hamstring and medial ligament trouble, he has always returned to first-team action. In August 1997 he became the club's most expensive sale when Crystal Palace paid £2 million. However, things did not go according to plan, for by March 1998 Palace still owed Wolves a lot of the money, letting him return to Molineux instead for £900,000. Now an important member of the Wolves' side, he has scored 10 goals – many of them vital – in 111 appearances for the Wanderers.

**EUROPEAN CUP** After receiving a bye in the first round of the 1958–59 European Cup competition, Wolves were drawn to play German side Schalke 04. A crowd of 45,767 saw the first leg at Molineux and, though Peter Broadbent scored twice for the home side, the game ended all square at 2–2. Facing an uphill struggle in the return leg, Wolves lost 2–1 and went out of the competition 4–3 on aggregate. The following season Wolves faced East German opposition in Vorwaerts in a preliminary round tie. Despite losing the first leg 2–1, goals from Broadbent and Mason in the return at Molineux gave the Midlands club a 3–2 win on aggregate. In the first round, Wolves were drawn to play Yugoslavian champions Red Star Belgrade. A Norman Deeley goal gave Wolves a 1–1 draw in front of 62,000 partisan fans in Belgrade before two goals from Bobby Mason and another from Jimmy Murray helped the Molineux club to a 3–0 home win and a place in the second round. Drawn against one of the best club sides of that day in Barcelona, Wolves were well beaten in both legs. At the Nou Camp Stadium, the Spanish giants won 4–0 before thrashing Wolves at Molineux 5–2 in front of a very disappointed crowd of 55,535.

**EUROPEAN CUP WINNERS' CUP** After beating Blackburn Rovers 3–0 in the 1960 FA Cup final, Wolves entered the European Cup Winners' Cup competition for the 1960–61 season. After receiving a bye in the qualifying round, the club went straight through to the quarter-final stage where they were drawn against FK Austria. Despite losing the first leg in Vienna 2–0, the Molineux club won their home leg 5–0 with Johnny Kirkham and Peter Broadbent netting two goals apiece. In the semi-final, Wolves played Glasgow Rangers but were always up against it after losing the first match 2–0 in front of an Ibrox crowd of almost 80,000. In the return, Broadbent was on target for Wolves but the Scottish side equalised to go through to the final 3–1 on aggregate.

**EVER-PRESENTS** Fifty-three Wolves players have been ever-presents throughout a Football League season. The greatest number of ever-present seasons by a Wolves player is five by Jack Jones. Next in line are Alf Bishop and Derek Parkin with four each.

**EVES, MEL** Wednesbury-born striker Mel Eves joined the club as an apprentice before turning professional in July 1975. He made his Wolves début in a goalless home draw against Ipswich Town in November 1977 and was an important member of the Molineux club for the next seven seasons. Eves, who won three England 'B' caps, also won a League Cup winners' medal in 1980 as Wolves beat Nottingham Forest 1–0. In 1982–83, when Wolves won promotion to the First Division, Eves was the club's top scorer with 19 goals. He went on to score 53 goals in 214 games before moving to Sheffield United after a loan spell at Huddersfield Town. In August 1986 the Bramall Lane club let him go to Gillingham. After just one season with the Kent club he had loan spells with Mansfield Town, Manchester City and West Bromwich Albion, though he failed to make the first teams of the last two clubs. He later played non-league football for Telford United and Cheltenham Town.

# F

**FA CUP** The club's first-ever FA Cup tie saw Wolves beat Long Eaton Rangers 4–1 on 27 October 1883. Their biggest victory in the competition came three seasons later when they beat Crosswell's Brewery 14–0 with Hunter, Brodie and Knight all scoring hat-tricks. In the next round of that season's competition, Wolves played Aston Villa and, after four gruelling matches, lost 2–0 to the eventual winners. Wolves reached the FA Cup final for the first time in 1889, losing 3–0 to Preston North End, the double-winners. The following season, Jack Brodie established the club's individual goalscoring record in the competition when he scored five goals in an 8–0 win over Stoke. Wolves first won the FA Cup in 1893 beating Everton 1–0 in the final at Fallowfield with captain Harry Allen the scorer. On the way they beat Bolton Wanderers 2–1 after a replay, Middlesbrough 2–1, Darwen 5–0 and Blackburn Rovers 2–1 in the semi-final at the Town Ground, Nottingham. Wolves reached the final again in 1896 but lost 2–1 to Sheffield Wednesday whose first goal came after just two minutes! The Molineux club won the FA Cup for a second time in 1908, beating Newcastle United 3–1 in the final at Crystal Palace with goals from Harrison, Hedley and Hunt. It was the first time since 1894 that a Second Division team had won the trophy. Wolves next reached the final in 1921 when they played Tottenham Hotspur at Stamford Bridge but, despite applying a lot of pressure, they lost 1–0. Wolves played in the 1939 FA Cup final, the last before the Second World War, but were well beaten 4–1 by Portsmouth. On their way to the final they beat Liverpool 4–1 in front of a record Molineux crowd of 61,315. Wolves won their first Wembley final in 1949 when they beat Leicester City 3–1 with Jesse Pye scoring two of the goals and Sammy Smyth one of the best individual goals seen at the famous ground. Wolves last played in an FA Cup final in 1960 when they defeated Blackburn Rovers 3–0. It

*FA Cup Postcard*

was a poor match marred by the injury to Rovers' full-back and now Wigan Athletic chairman, Dave Whelan. Wolves have also appeared in 14 FA Cup semi-finals, the last occasion being 5 April 1998 when they lost 1–0 to Arsenal at Villa Park.

**FA CUP FINALS** Wolverhampton Wanderers have appeared in eight FA Cup finals, winning the trophy on four occasions:

| | | |
|---|---|---|
| 1889 | v Preston North End (Kennington Oval) | 0–3 |
| 1893 | v Everton (Fallowfield) | 1–0 |
| 1896 | v Sheffield Wednesday (Crystal Palace) | 1–2 |
| 1908 | v Newcastle United (Crystal Palace) | 3–1 |
| 1921 | v Tottenham Hotspur (Stamford Bridge) | 0–1 |
| 1939 | v Portsmouth (Wembley) | 1–4 |
| 1949 | v Leicester City (Wembley) | 3–1 |
| 1960 | v Blackburn Rovers (Wembley) | 3–0 |

**FA CUP SEMI-FINALS** Wolverhampton Wanderers have participated in 14 FA Cup semi-finals up to the end of the 1998–99 season.

**FARMER, TED** Wolves' scouts had taken careful note of Ted Farmer's goalscoring exploits and in the summer of 1956 he joined the Molineux club as an amateur. In his first season playing for the Wolves junior team, he scored a remarkable 86 goals and in August 1957 he was signed up as a professional by manager Stan Cullis. Farmer made his Wolves début against Manchester United at Old Trafford and scored twice in a 3–1 win. After that there was no stopping him and on his first season on the side he scored 28 goals in 27 league games including 4 in a 5–1 home win over Birmingham City and he put a hat-trick in a 5–3 defeat of Arsenal. His performances led to his winning two caps for England at Under-23 level against Israel and Holland and a hat-trick past the Dutch. Farmer scored four goals for Wolves on the opening day of the 1962–63 season as Manchester City were beaten 8–1. However, the Molineux club were robbed of the services of this great goalscorer after just six games of the 1963–64 season when injury ended Ted Farmer's career at the age of 24. He had scored 44 goals in 57 League games.

**FATHER AND SON** One of the most famous father and son combinations is that of Dicky Baugh senior and Dicky Baugh junior.

Dicky Baugh senior played in three FA Cup finals for Wolves, was capped twice by England and appeared in 227 first-team games. His son Dicky Baugh junior, also a full-back, played in 120 games for Wolves before moving to West Bromwich Albion.

**FAZACKERLY, STAN** After an unsuccessful trial with his home-town club Preston North End, inside-forward Stan Fazackerly began his career with Accrington Stanley, then members of the Lancashire Combination. In April 1912 he joined Hull City before moving to Sheffield United 12 months later for a fee of £1,000. He appeared for the Blades in the 1915 FA Cup final and scored one of their goals in a 3–0 win over Chelsea. In November 1920, Everton paid a British-record fee of £4,000 for his services but two years later, after scoring 21 goals in 57 games for the Goodison Park club, he arrived at Molineux along with fellow Everton player George Brewster. He made his début for Wolves in a 3–1 home win over Stockport County in November 1922 and in the following season he was a key member of the Wolves side that won the Third Division (North) Championship. In that campaign he scored 14 goals in 38 games including a hat-trick in a 5–1 home win over his former club, Accrington Stanley. At the end of the 1924–25 season, Fazackerly, who had scored 32 goals in 77 games, left to join Derby County. He spent just one season at the Baseball Ground before retiring on medical advice.

**FERGUSON, DARREN** The son of Manchester United manager Alex Ferguson, Darren came through the ranks at Old Trafford before making his league début at Sheffield United in February 1991. The following season he played for the Scotland Under-21 side and was called up for the annual end-of-season tournament in Toulon. In 1992–93 he won a League Championship medal as United raced away to win the Premiership – and it was one of the few occasions that a player has won an award while playing for a team managed by his father. In January 1994 he left Old Trafford to join Wolverhampton Wanderers for a fee of £250,000 and made his début in a 2–0 home win over Crystal Palace. Though he is capable of producing defence-splitting passes, he has, on occasion, let his temper get the better of him, and sendings-off and bookings have produced a number of suspensions which have reduced his appearances in almost five years at Molineux to 143.

**FINLAYSON, MALCOLM** Wolves boss Stan Cullis paid Third Division Millwall £4,000 for the services of Malcolm Finlayson in the summer of 1956. The Dumbarton-born keeper had played in 229 league games for the Lions and was signed by the Molineux club as a replacement for the great Bert Williams. Finlayson made his League début for the Wanderers in a 2–1 home defeat by Leeds United on 15 September 1956 but had to wait until after the start of the 1957–58 season before becoming the club's first-choice keeper. At the end of that campaign, Finlayson had conceded just 40 goals in 37 games and won a League Championship medal. A second League Championship medal came his way in 1958–59 and the following season he kept a clean sheet as Wolves beat Blackburn Rovers 3–0 to win the FA Cup final at Wembley. Towards the end of his career, Finlayson suffered a number of injury problems and, after appearing in 203 league and cup games for the club, gave way to Fred Davies. Finlayson's last game for Wolves came in a 6–0 defeat against Liverpool at Anfield in September 1963, 15 years after he had turned professional. On his retirement he went into business developing a number of foundries throughout the Midlands. In June 1982 he was appointed vice-chairman of Wolverhampton Wanderers, though sadly the appointment was short-lived as a new regime took charge of the club.

**FIRST DIVISION** Wolves have had six spells in the First Division. Following their admission to the Football League in 1888, Wolves played in the top flight for 18 seasons before experiencing their first relegation in 1905–06. During that time, the club's highest position had been third in seasons 1888–89 and 1897–98. The club's second spell in the First Division was their longest, stretching 26 seasons from 1932–33 to 1964–65. Wolves won the League Championship in seasons 1953–54, 1957–58 and 1958–59 and were runners-up on a further five occasions. After two seasons of Second Division football, Wolves embarked on their third spell of top flight football but in 1975–76 the club were relegated after spending the last nine seasons in the First Division. This time the club won the Second Division at the first attempt to begin their fourth spell of top flight football in 1977–78. There then followed a series of relegations, after the club lost its First Division status in 1981–82, that saw them play two seasons of Fourth Division football. The club eventually returned to the Second Division in 1989–90 but since reorganisation in 1992–93 Wolves have played seven seasons in the 'new' First Division in what is their sixth spell.

**FIRST LEAGUE MATCH** Wolves' first Football League match saw them entertain Aston Villa at Dudley Road on 8 September 1888. Wolves kicked downhill in the first half, the sun on their backs, but the strong wind against them. Early on, Wolves' forwards Anderson and Cannon both came close to scoring, the former hitting an upright with Warner in the Villa goal well beaten. Villa, too, came close to opening the scoring, with both Brown and Garvey missing easy chances. Jack Baynton, the Wolves keeper, denied Green with a last-ditch dive at the Villa man's feet. However, it was Wolves who opened the scoring on the half-hour when White put in a header from Hunter's cross. Villa's full-back Gersh Cox tried to clear his lines but only succeeded in turning the ball into his own goal to put Wolves 1–0 up. Villa hit back and drew level just before half-time when Tommy Green drove Garvey's pass over the line via the upright. In the second half, Wolves had the better chances but Cooper and Hunter had shots saved by Warner, and Anderson missed a sitter from just five yards out. This was a very sporting local derby, fast and furious throughout, with a draw the fair result. The Wolves team that day was: Baynton; Mason; Baugh; Fletcher; Allen; Lowder; Hunter; Cooper; Anderson; Cannon; and White.

**FIRST MATCH** The club were known as St Luke's when they played their first match on 13 January 1877. Their opponents that day were undoubtedly the best team in Wolverhampton, Stafford Road FC. A crowd of around 600 watched a fairly one-sided match on a piece of land near the town's orphanage and saw Stafford Road win 8–0. The St Luke's side was: Barcroft; Hampton; Hedges; Adams; Rowbotham; Worrall; Kendrick; Baynton; Newman; Myatt; Jacks; and Foster.

**FLEMING, GEORGE** Born in Bannockburn, tough-tackling left-half George Fleming joined Wolves from East Stirlingshire in 1894 and made his début in a 3–1 home defeat by Preston North End on the opening day of the 1894–95 season. Fleming missed very few games over the next seven seasons, though one he did fail to play in was the 1896 FA Cup final defeat by Sheffield Wednesday. He was an ever-present in 1897–98 when Wolves finished third in Division One and again the following two seasons, appearing in 117 consecutive League games. He had appeared in 187 games for Wolves when he lost his place to Jack Whitehouse and joined Liverpool. He made 83 League appearances for the Anfield club and won a Second Division Championship medal before becoming the Merseyside club's assistant-trainer.

**FLOODLIGHTS** The first floodlit game at Molineux was a friendly match against a South African XI on 30 September 1953, watched by a crowd of 33,681. In that game, Wolves played in luminous shirts under a floodlighting system of just 60 lamps, costing only 7s 6d (38 pence) to run. There then followed a series of floodlit friendlies against such clubs as Honved, Spartak Moscow, Racing Club of Buenos Aires and First Vienna (see Floodlit Encounters), despite local cinema owners complaining that these matches were harming their business! The club's floodlights were quite low and four years later they were replaced by a much taller set costing £25,000.

**FLOODLIT ENCOUNTERS** After floodlights had been installed at Molineux, Wolves embarked on a series of floodlit matches, beating Racing Club of Buenos Aires 3–1, Moscow Dynamo 2–1 and Spartak Moscow 4–0, but of all their floodlit fixtures against foreign opposition, the match against the top Hungarian side Honved was the one that mattered. Hungary, led by Ferenc Puskas, had beaten England 6–3 at Wembley in November 1953 and the following summer emphasised their superiority by winning 7–1 in Budapest. So with English football at a low ebb, the match between Wolves and Honved took on a new meaning. The Hungarians came to Molineux on 13 December 1954, fielding five of the players who had humiliated England. Of the Wolves team, only Billy Wright, the captain, had been on the receiving end of those two heavy international defeats. Wolves wore a special satin version of the gold shirt which they believed would look better under floodlights. However, after a quarter of an hour Honved were two goals up through Kocsis and Machos and, as the Hungarians pressed forward in search of a third goal, both forwards brought fine saves out of Wolves keeper Bert Williams. Early in the second-half, Johnny Hancocks reduced the arrears when Wolves were awarded a penalty. Then, with 54,998 fans cheering them on, Roy Swinbourne scored two goals in the space of a minute. Molineux went wild, as did the

*Programme Cover*

thousands who had watched the game on television: Wolves had beaten the mighty Honved 3–2.

**FLOWERS, RON** Born at Edlington, near Doncaster, Ron Flowers joined the Wolves nursery side, Wath Wanderers, in the summer of 1950 before turning professional two years later. He made his début in September 1952 at home to Blackpool and, though the Seasiders won 5–2, Flowers headed one of Wolves' goals. After helping the Molineux club win the League Championship in 1953–54, he began to produce performances that led to his winning the first of 49 caps for England when he played against France in May 1955. His last game in an England shirt came 11 years later in a 6–1 win over Norway, a year in which he was a member of England's World Cup 40. Flowers won further League Championship medals in 1957–58 and 1958–59 and in 1960 won an FA Cup winners' medal when Wolves beat Blackburn Rovers 3–0. He spent 15 years as a professional at Molineux and scored 37 goals in 512 games before joining Northampton Town in September 1967. He later became player-coach of the Cobblers before becoming player-manager of non-League Wellington Town. By the time he had guided them to the FA Trophy final they had been renamed Telford United, but in 1971 he left the club to run his own sports shop in Wolverhampton.

**FLOWERS, TIM** England international goalkeeper Tim Flowers began his League career with Wolverhampton Wanderers, making his début at home to Sheffield United in August 1984. Although he conceded two goals in a 2–2 draw, he showed great potential and went on to play in 38 League games that season. However, the club were relegated to the Third Division and in 1985–86 relegated yet again, this time to the Fourth Division. He had appeared in 72 first team games for Wolves when he went on loan to Southampton, and he didn't play a match for them before signing for the Saints as Peter Shilton's understudy. He made a less than auspicious start, conceding five goals on his First Division début at Old Trafford. In his second game against Arsenal he fractured a cheekbone and had two loan spells at Swindon Town before breaking into the Southampton side on a regular basis. After missing just five games between 1989–90 and 1991–92, he was ever-present in 1992–93 at the end of which he won his first England cap in a 1–1 draw against a good Brazilian side in the USA Cup match. A good shot-stopper and possessing great concentration, he had played in 234 League and Cup games for the Saints when he was transferred to Blackburn Rovers for £2.4 million in November 1993. In 1994–95 he helped the Ewood Park club win the Premier League Championship and is a regular member of the England squad, having won 10 international caps.

**FOOTBALL LEAGUE CUP** Though the competition was introduced in 1960, Wolves, like a number of other First Division clubs, refused to enter during its early years. Their first game was against Mansfield Town at Molineux on 13 September 1966 when goals from Hatton and Wharton gave them a 2–1 win before they went out to Fulham in the next round. In 1972–73, Wolves beat Orient (Home 2–1) Sheffield Wednesday (Home 3–1) Bristol Rovers (Home 4–0) and Blackpool (Away 1–0 after a 1–1 draw at Molineux) before losing 4–3 after extra time to Tottenham Hotspur in the two-legged semi-final. The following season Wolves won the League Cup for the first time, beating Manchester City 2–1 in the final with goals from Hibbitt and Richards, though goalkeeper Gary Pierce was named 'Man of the Match'. On their way to the final, Wolves had beaten Tranmere Rovers (Home 2–1 after a 1–1 draw at Prenton Park), Exeter City (Home 5–1), Liverpool (Home 1–0) and Norwich City 2–1 on aggregate in the semi-final. Wolves won the League Cup again in 1980 when an Andy Gray goal was enough to beat Nottingham Forest, who had won the trophy for the last two seasons.

**FOOTBALLER OF THE YEAR** The Football Writers' Association Award for the Footballer of the Year has been won by Wolverhampton Wanderers players on two occasions: Billy Wright (1951–52) and Bill Slater (1959–60).

**FORMATION** Wolverhampton Wanderers Football Club came into being in 1879 when players from St Luke's, which was founded in 1877, and Goldthorn, founded in 1876, broke away to form the present club.

**FOURTH DIVISION** Wolves have had just one spell of two seasons in the Fourth Division following their relegation to the league's basement at the end of the 1985–86 campaign. After a mixed start to the 1986–87 season, which included the club losing to non-league Chorley in the FA Cup first round, Wolves began to string together a run of good results and when they won 11 of their last 12 games, they reached the divisional play-offs. In that sequence, the club conceded just six goals, three of them coming at Halifax Town where Wolves won a seven-goal thriller. After beating Colchester United in the play-off semi-final, Wolves lost 3–0 on aggregate to Aldershot and lost the chance of making an immediate return to the Third Division. In 1987–88, Wolves played some magnificent football to take the Fourth Division Championship and the Sherpa Van Trophy and, in doing so, became the first club to win all four divisions of the Football League. They finished the season five points ahead of runners-up Cardiff City and Steve Bull scored 34 of the club's 82 league goals.

**FREIGHT ROVER TROPHY** A competition designed solely and specifically for Associate Members of the Football League, the Freight Rover Trophy replaced the initial Associate Members' Cup for the 1984–85 season. Wolves first participated in the competition in 1985–86 after drawing both their group matches against Exeter City (Away 1–1) and Torquay United (Home 1–1), but they failed to qualify for the knockout stages. In 1986–87, Wolves won both their group matches, 1–0 at Cardiff City and 4–3 at home to Bournemouth, a match in which Steve Bull and Paul Dougherty scored two goals apiece. In the first round, the Molineux club lost 1–0 at home to Hereford United.

**FROGGATT, STEPHEN** Left-winger Stephen Froggatt made his Aston Villa début as a substitute on Boxing Day 1991 in a 3–1 home win over West Ham United. He subsequently enjoyed a short run in the first team and in 1992–93 was capped by England at Under-21 level. That season he appeared in almost every game until sustaining an ankle injury at Wimbledon. He came back but the injury got the better of him and after playing in 44 League and Cup games for Villa, he signed for Wolverhampton Wanderers in July 1994 for a fee of £1 million. He scored the only goal of the game on his début against Reading on the opening day of the 1994–95 season but midway through the campaign a serious ankle injury halted his progress. Though he returned to the Wolves side in 1995–96 he found himself tiring easily and it was only after the

*Stephen Froggatt*

ailment was diagnosed as a blood clot that he returned to his true form six months later. In fact, he moved to play wing-back in 1996–97 and, though injuries sadly continued to interrupt his career, he was elected by his fellow professionals in the PFA award-winning First Division side. After that, the left-footed Froggatt seemed to be used anywhere on that side and had taken his appearances for the Molineux club to 111 before joining Coventry City.

# G

**GALLEY, TOM** A part-time professional with Cannock, Tom Galley joined Wolves in August 1933 and signed professional forms eight months later. He made his début in a goalless draw at Sunderland in January 1935. After that he missed very few matches up to the outbreak of the Second World War and was ever-present in 1938–39 when he had his best season in terms of goals scored, finding the net on 11 occasions. Including the war years, Tom Galley spent 13 seasons at Molineux and occupied seven different positions, though his best position was always thought to be right-half. He won two England caps whilst with Wolves, winning his first against Norway in May 1937, and appeared for the Molineux club in the 1939 FA Cup final against Portsmouth. During the hostilities, Galley captained Wolves to victory in the 1942 Wartime Cup final over Sunderland and went on to appear in 75 games. When League football resumed in 1946–47, Galley lined up at right-half but in November 1947, after scoring 49 goals in 204 League and Cup games, he left Molineux to captain Grimsby Town. Sadly after just 33 League appearances for the Mariners, injury forced him to quit League football. He then had a spell with Kidderminster Harriers before joining Clacton Town as player-coach.

**GARDINER, JOE** Born in the same Durham mining village, Bearpark, as the great Derby County and England winger, Sammy Crooks, Joe Gardiner joined Wolves as an amateur in January 1932. However, he had to wait until 23 February 1935 before making his first-team début in a Wolves side that went down 5–2 at West Bromwich Albion. It was towards the end of the following season that he won a regular place in the side, his performances earning him a call up to the Football League XI for their match against the Scottish League in 1937–38. Gardiner was also a member of the

Wolves side that lost 4–1 to Portsmouth in the 1939 FA Cup final at Wembley. When he arrived at Molineux, Joe Gardiner was tried at centre-forward but after being switched to half-back he gave the club great service, scoring six goals in 192 league and cup games. After retiring in 1944 he stayed on at Molineux for a further ten years as coach-trainer. In 1954 he followed his manager Stan Cullis to Birmingham City where he stayed for another ten years, during which time he acted as trainer to the full England team on two occasions.

**GARRATLY, GEORGE** Full-back George Garratly was playing for Bloxwich Strollers when Walsall signed him in February 1908. After a number of impressive performances for the Saddlers in the Birmingham League, Wolves signed him in the summer of 1909 and he made his début on 27 November 1909 in a 2–0 home defeat by Bradford. He was ever-present in seasons 1910–11 and 1911–12 and appeared in 97 consecutive league games. He formed a good full-back pairing with Ted Collins, thought to be the best outside the top flight. Despite his career being interrupted by the First World War, Garratly was still a member of the Wolves first team after the hostilities were over. He appeared in 238 games for Wolves before ending his career in non-league football with Hednesford Town.

**GEORGE, NOEL** Goalkeeper Noel George began his career as a forward with Hednesford before the First World War but, during the hostilities while serving in France and Salonika, he took up goalkeeping. Wolves signed him in the summer of 1919 and he made his League début for the Molineux club in a 1–1 draw at Nottingham Forest on 5 February 1921. After making eight appearances that season, George became the club's first-choice keeper at the start of the 1921–22 campaign, having played in the previous season's FA Cup final defeat by Tottenham Hotspur at Stamford Bridge. An ever-present in seasons 1921–22, 1923–24 and 1924–25, he missed very few games during his seven seasons in the Wolves' side. When Wolves won the Third Division (North) Championship in 1923–24, George conceded just 31 goals in 47 League and Cup games and kept a record 25 clean sheets. The popular keeper had played in 13 games of the 1927–28 season when he was diagnosed as having an incurable disease. The first sign of his illness came in a 4–0 defeat at Bristol City in November 1927, his last game for the club, and although he battled hard to overcome the illness, he slowly got worse and passed away in his sleep at Lichfield in October 1929 when he was only 31 years old.

**GOALKEEPERS** Wolverhampton Wanderers FC has almost always been extremely well served by its goalkeepers and most of them have been highly popular with their supporters. Whilst Isaac Griffiths was the first recognised goalkeeper to stand between the posts for Wolverhampton Wanderers, Jack Baynton was the last line of defence during the club's first Football League campaign of 1888–89. He was also a splendid utility player and captained the club on a number of occasions. He once scored a goal when he fly-kicked the ball in a local cup tie from fully 100 yards – and somehow it found its way into the opposition goal! The club's first international goalkeeper was Billy Rose, who was replaced by Billy Tennent who kept goal in the 1896 FA Cup final against Sheffield Wednesday. Tom Baddeley, who spent 11 years at Molineux, was also an England international and appeared in 315 games for Wolves. Welsh international keeper Teddy Peers never actually wanted to be a goalkeeper but he turned out to be one of the finest in the country in the years either side of the First World War. One of the best of Wolves' goalkeepers was Noel George, who took up the position while serving in the army. He played in a total of 242 League and Cup games before his untimely death at the age of 31. Alf Tootill, who was nicknamed 'The Birdcatcher', won a Second Division Championship medal in 1931–32. He was a small acrobatic keeper who later played for Fulham and Crystal Palace. Bert Williams, who won 24 caps for England, was the club's first-choice keeper for 12 seasons during which time he appeared in 448 games. He played for England in the 1950 World Cup and was only on the losing side in seven of his matches. Malcolm Finlayson, Williams' replacement, played in 203 games and was between the posts when Wolves beat Blackburn Rovers 3–0 to win the FA Cup in 1960. One of the club's tallest goalkeepers was Phil Parkes, who made 127 consecutive League appearances to break Noel George's record. Only Bert Williams has played in more games as a goalkeeper than the West Bromwich-born keeper. Paul Bradshaw was Wolves' record signing when he joined the club from Blackburn Rovers for a fee of £150,000 in September 1977, and went on to play in 243 games. The club's present custodian is Mike Stowell, who at the time of writing has appeared in 366 games since his début in March 1989.

**GOALS** The greatest number of goals Wolverhampton Wanderers have ever scored in one game was in their 14–0 victory over Crosswell's Brewery in the second round of the FA Cup on 13 November 1886. In the Football League, Wolves beat Leicester City 10–1 at Molineux on 15 April 1937 and on 3 September 1955 travelled to Ninian Park where they beat Cardiff City 9–1.

**GOALS – CAREER BEST** The highest goalscorer in the club's history is Steve Bull, who between seasons 1986–87 and 1997–98 netted 300 goals. These comprised 246 in the League, 7 in the FA Cup, 15 in the Football League Cup and 32 in other competitions.

**GOALS – INDIVIDUAL** Four players have scored five goals in a match for Wolverhampton Wanderers, though Billy Hartill achieved the feat on two occasions. The first player to score five goals for the club was Jack Brodie in the third round FA Cup game against Stoke on 22 February 1890, which Wolves won 8–0. The first Wolves player to achieve the feat in the Football League was Joe Butcher, who netted all Wolves' goals in a 5–3 win over Accrington on 19 November 1892. The feat was next achieved on Christmas Day 1926 when Tom Phillipson scored five goals in the 7–2 win over Bradford City. Billy Hartill netted five goals in a match on two occasions – the first in a 5–1 win over Notts County on 12 October 1929 and then again on 3 September 1934 as Aston Villa were beaten 5–2 in a First Division encounter.

**GOALS – SEASON** The club's highest league goalscorer in any one season remains Dennis Westcott, who scored 38 league goals as Wolves finished third in Division One in 1946–47. The season's highest tally for all matches is the 52 goals achieved by Steve Bull. Thirty-four were scored in the League, three in the FA Cup, three in the League Cup and 12 in the Sherpa Van Trophy.

**GOODMAN, DON** Leeds-born forward Don Goodman played his early football with Collingham before entering league football with Bradford City. He had scored 22 goals in 86 games for the Valley Parade club and helped them win the Third Division Championship when he joined West Bromwich Albion for £50,000 in March 1987. At The Hawthorns, Goodman continued to score on a regular basis and had netted 63 in 181 league and cup games when Sunderland paid £900,000 for his services in December 1991. His début for the Wearsiders was in a 1–0 defeat at Wolverhampton Wanderers, the day after signing for the north-east club. In only his seventh game for the club, he netted a hat-trick in a 6–2 home win over Millwall and continued to find the net with great regularity. He had scored 47 goals in 133 first-team outings when in December 1994 he joined Wolverhampton Wanderers for £1.1 million. After making his début in a 1–0 home win over Notts County, he found himself playing behind Steve Bull and David Kelly, but having replaced the Republic of Ireland international, he demonstrated his goalscoring talents with 10 goals in a 13-match spell in 1995–96 and ended the campaign as the club's leading scorer with 20 league and cup goals. In April 1996 he fractured his skull but made a remarkable recovery to return to first-team action. He scored the winning goal against Leeds United in the quarter-final of the 1997–98 FA Cup competition and looked most likely to score against Arsenal in the semi-final before surprisingly being released in the summer after scoring 39 goals in 154 games for the Molineux club.

**GOULD, BOBBY** A much-travelled striker and great-hearted competitor, Bobby Gould began his career with his home-town club Coventry City. After scoring 40 goals in 82 league games and helping the Sky Blues win promotion to the First Division, he moved to Arsenal and was in the Gunners side that lost to Third Division Swindon Town in the League Cup final of 1969. He joined Wolves in the summer of 1970 and made his début in a 3–2 defeat at Newcastle United on the opening day of the 1970–71 season. He ended the campaign as the club's leading scorer with 24 league and cup goals including netting a hat-trick in a 3–2 home win over Manchester United. After scoring in the opening game of the following season, he appeared in just five more games before joining West Bromwich Albion. He scored 18 goals in 52 games for the Baggies before being transferred to Bristol City. In November 1973 he signed for West Ham United. He scored a hat-trick in a 6–0 League Cup win over Tranmere Rovers and was instrumental in the Hammers reaching the 1975 FA Cup final. In December 1975 he rejoined Wolves and the following season scored ten league goals in

*Bobby Gould*

11 starts. Gould scored 39 goals in 93 games for Wolves during his two spells with the club before playing for Bristol Rovers and Hereford United. He later became manager at Eastville and, after a spell in charge at Coventry City, he returned to take over the reins at Bristol Rovers again before leading Wimbledon to their shock 1988 FA Cup final success over Liverpool. He moved back to

*Andy Gray*

Highfield Road in 1992 after an unhappy spell in charge of West Bromwich Albion and until very recently was manager of Wales.

**GRAY, ANDY** One of the bravest strikers of his generation, Andy Gray began his career with Dundee United, scoring 44 goals in 76 games for the Tannadice club. He signed for Aston Villa for £110,000 in September 1975. In 1976–77, Villa finished fourth in the First Division and beat Everton in the final of the League Cup. Gray was the club's top scorer with 29 goals in 48 appearances and was voted the PFA Player of the Year and Young Player of the Year. After four years at Villa Park he moved to Wolverhampton Wanderers for a British record fee of £1.5 million. He scored on his Wolves début in September 1979 in a 3–2 win at Everton. Towards the end of his first season at Molineux he scored perhaps his most treasured goal, the winner in the League Cup final against Nottingham Forest. Injuries then ruined the rest of his time with Wolves and in November 1983, after scoring 45 goals in 162 games, he joined Everton for £250,000. He ended his first season with the Goodison club scoring the Blues' second goal in the 1984 FA Cup final win over Watford. He also scored the opening goal in the 1985 European Cup Winners' Cup triumph over Rapid Vienna and at the end of the season was dramatically recalled into the Scotland side, eventually ending up with 20 full caps to his name. He had scored 22 goals in 68 games when he rejoined Villa for £150,000. After a loan spell at Notts County, he signed for West Bromwich Albion but retired shortly after his arrival at The Hawthorns. In the summer of 1991 he returned to Villa Park for a third time as assistant-manager to Ron Atkinson. He resigned in 1992 to pursue a career in television with Sky.

**GREAVES, IAN** Ian Greaves joined Manchester United in the early 1950s but being a defender he found it difficult to displace players of the calibre of Roger Byrne, Bill Foulkes and Duncan Edwards, so his first-team opportunities were rare. He did win a League Championship medal in 1955–56 by appearing in the last 14 games of the season but it was the Munich air crash which provided the unhappy opening for his breakthrough. He played in the 1958 FA Cup final but after 75 appearances for United he moved to Lincoln City before ending his playing career with Oldham Athletic. His first managerial post was with Huddersfield Town and in 1970 he took the Terriers to the Second Division title. After two seasons in the top flight, the Yorkshire club suffered successive relegations to the Third Division, and after a boardroom struggle, he walked out to take charge at Bolton Wanderers. He took the Trotters to the semi-finals of the League Cup in 1977 and the following season to

*Ian Greaves*

the Second Division Championship. In January 1980, with Bolton firmly rooted to the foot of the First Division, he was dismissed. After a spell in charge of Oxford United, he became manager of Wolverhampton Wanderers. Although he was highly regarded by the club's supporters, he failed to halt the Wanderers' decline. After only five wins in six months at Molineux, he was sacked by the new regime led by Derek Dougan. In 1983 he became manager of Mansfield Town, leading them to promotion and victory at Wembley in the Freight Rover Trophy Final.

**GREGORY, VAL** Aggressive wing-half Val Gregory, who captained Wolves in the 1921 FA Cup final against Tottenham Hotspur, played his early football with Reading and Watford before appearing for Arsenal during the First World War. He joined Wolverhampton Wanderers in May 1920 and made his début in a 2–0 defeat at Fulham on the opening day of the 1920–21 season. That campaign saw him score his only two goals for the club, each proving to be the winning goal in an away game – Port Vale (3–2) and Hull City (1–0). He was a virtual ever-present in his three seasons with the club and had appeared in 106 games when he retired at the end of the 1922–23 campaign. He then became coach and later trainer at Molineux before ill health forced him to sever his connections with the club in 1938.

**GRIFFIN, ALF** Outside-left Alf Griffin played his early football with Brierley Hill and his home-town club Walsall before signing for Wolves in the summer of 1892. He made his début at Newton Heath on 15 October 1892, a game Wolves lost 10–1, and went straight back into the club's reserve side. However, towards the end of that season he was given another chance and, after scoring in the 5–0 FA Cup third-round win over Darwen, kept his place and won an FA Cup winners' medal as Wolves beat Everton 1–0. He scored 14 goals in 76 games for Wolves before being transferred back to Walsall in 1896. He took his tally of goals for the Saddlers to 34 in 88 games in his two spells before a bad ankle injury ended his career.

**GROVES, ALBERT** One of the smallest centre-halves ever to play for the club, Albert Groves joined Wolves from Aberdeen in the summer of 1909 and made his début in a 3–2 home win over Manchester City on the final day of the 1909–10 season. After that,

Groves, who played in a variety of positions for the club, missed very few matches in the five seasons leading up to the First World War. In 1912–13 he scored ten goals in 37 games as he turned out for the club at inside-forward. After playing in Midland Victory League matches during the 1918–19 season, he had one more season of league football before trying his luck in management. Groves had scored 20 goals in 217 league and cup games when he was appointed player-manager of Walsall, a position he held for just one season before becoming secretary at Fellows Park.

**GUEST PLAYERS** The guest system was used by all clubs during both world wars. Although on occasions it was abused almost beyond belief (some sides that opposed Wolves had ten or 11 guests!) it normally worked sensibly and effectively and to the benefit of players, clubs and supporters. Whilst Wolves' Stan Cullis joined Everton's Cliff Bitton and Joe Mercer to make Aldershot one of the strongest wartime teams with the England half-back line on call, Wolves themselves had a number of famous 'guests' including England internationals Neil Franklin and Jack Rowley. The Manchester United forward, Jack Rowley, whom Wolves once let go to Bournemouth, scored five in an 11–1 win over Everton and all eight when Derby County were beaten 8–1 in November 1942.

# H

**HALLIGAN, BILLY** Irish international forward Billy Halligan began his career with Belfast Distillery before later playing for Belfast Celtic and Cliftonville. In 1909 he joined Leeds United and scored twice on his début in a 5–0 win over Lincoln City. He had scored 12 goals in 24 games when in February 1910 he left to sign for Derby County, but a little over a year later he joined Wolverhampton Wanderers for a fee of £450. His first game in the Molineux club's colours was in the goalless draw at Grimsby Town on the opening day of the 1911–12 season. He was the club's top scorer that season with 24 goals in 39 league and cup games including hat-tricks against Hull City (Home 8–0) Barnsley (Home 5–0) and Watford (Home 10–0), the latter being an FA Cup first round replay. He top-scored again in 1912–13 with 17 goals in 34 games including scoring in five consecutive league games. He had scored 41 goals in 73 first team outings when he left Molineux to join Hull City for what was then the Yorkshire club's record fee of £600. He had netted 28 goals in 64 games for the Tigers when the First World War interrupted his career. During the hostilities he guested for Manchester United and Rochdale before signing for Preston North End in July 1919. On leaving Deepdale he had spells with Oldham Athletic and Nelson before playing non-league football for both Boston Town and Wisbech Town.

**HANCOCKS, JOHNNY** Goalscoring winger Johnny Hancocks began his league career with Walsall but in May 1946 Wolves paid £4,000 to bring him to Molineux and he made his début in the 6–1 win over Arsenal on the opening day of the 1946–47 season. The following season he was the club's joint top scorer with 16 goals, and in 1949 he won an FA Cup winners' medal as Wolves beat Leicester City 3–1 at Wembley. His form that season had led to him winning the first of three full caps for England when he scored twice in a 6–0 win over Switzerland. He netted his first hat-trick for Wolves in December 1950 in a 3–1 home win over West Bromwich Albion and his second during the club's League Championship-winning season of 1953–54 when Wolves beat Chelsea 8–1. The following season, Hancocks was the club's leading scorer with 26 goals in 32 games including hat-tricks against Huddersfield Town (Home 6–4) and Arsenal (Home 3–1). Hancocks topped the goalscoring charts again in 1955–56 when his total of 18 goals in 28 games included his fifth and final hat-trick for the club in a 9–1 win at Cardiff City. Sadly it was his last season in the first team and, after scoring 168 goals in 378 league and cup games, he spent a season in the club's Central League side before becoming player-manager of Wellington Town. He later ended his career with Cambridge United, who were then members of the Southern League, Oswestry and GKN Sankey.

**HARRINGTON, JACK** One of the fastest wingers ever to play for Wolves, Jack Harrington made his first-team début in a goalless draw at Chesterfield on the first day of the 1923–24 season. He went on to score three goals in 27 games but made many more for Lees and Phillipson as Wolves won the Third Division (North) Championship. Harrington was a regular in the Wolves side for the next five seasons, scoring 10 goals in 117 games as the club consolidated their position in the higher division. After leaving Molineux in the summer of 1928, he had a season with Northampton Town but was hampered by a series of injuries and a loss of form and left to play non–league football with Brierley Hill Alliance.

**HARRIS, GERRY** After turning down the offer of a trial with West Bromwich Albion, left-back Gerry Harris joined Wolves in 1954 after impressing for Bobbington FC in the Wolverhampton Amateur League. He had to wait until August 1956 before making his début in a nine-goal thriller as Wolves beat Luton Town 5–4 in front of a Molineux crowd of 46,781. He played in 31 league games that campaign and won League Championship medals in consecutive seasons as Wolves won the title in 1957–58 and 1958–59. The strong-tackling defender won four caps for England at Under-23 level and won an FA Cup winners' medal in 1960 when Blackburn Rovers were beaten 3–0 in the Wembley final. Harris stayed with Wolves until 1966 when, after 270 first-team appearances, he joined Walsall. After just one season with the Saddlers, however, he hung up his boots.

**HARRISON, BILLY** Winger Billy Harrison began his career playing in the Birmingham and District League for Crewe Alexandra before joining Wolves in the summer of 1907. He played his first game for the club in a 2–1 home defeat by West Bromwich Albion on the opening day of the 1907–08 season and went on to score four goals in 31 league games. Also that season he won an FA Cup winners' medal, scoring one of the goals in the 3–1 defeat of Newcastle United in the final at the Crystal Palace. All of Harrison's league appearances for Wolves were in the Second Division and by the time he left to join Manchester United in October 1920 he had scored 49 goals in 345 first-team games. He made 46 appearances for the Old Trafford club before moving to Port Vale and later Wrexham, where he ended his league career.

**HARTILL, BILLY** Nicknamed 'Artillery', Billy Hartill joined the Royal Horse Artillery on leaving school and in his two seasons for the Army team scored over 70 goals. When he was demobbed in the summer of 1928, he joined Wolverhampton Wanderers and in November of that year made his début at Bradford. The following season, Hartill was the club's leading scorer with 33 goals in 35 league games, a total which included all five goals in a 5–1 defeat of Notts County and hat-tricks against Preston North End (Home 4–0) and Bradford (Home 4–4). He was the club's top scorer again in 1930–31 with 30 league and cup goals. He scored four goals in the 9–1 FA Cup third round victory over Wrexham and netted hat-tricks in the league against Stoke (Home 5–1), Bury (Home 7–0) and Bristol City (Away 3–0). When Wolves won the Second Division Championship in 1931–32, Hartill was not only the club's leading scorer with 30 goals in 38 league games but, he also scored four hat-tricks against Millwall (Home 5–0), Bristol City (Home 4–2), Southampton (Home 5–1) and Oldham Athletic (Home 7–1). He also topped the club's scoring charts in 1932–33 and 1934–35 but in the summer of 1935, after netting 16 hat-tricks in his total of 170 goals in 234 games, he left Molineux to join Everton. He later played for Liverpool and Bristol City – though never in the Ashton Gate club's first team – before injury forced his retirement in 1940.

**HAT-TRICKS** The first Wolves player to score a hat-trick in the Football League was Harry Wood in the match against Derby County on 3 November 1888. The most hat-tricks in one match is three when Wolves beat Crosswell's Brewery 14–0 in a second round tie in 1886–87. The three players to score hat-tricks were Tom Hunter (4), Jack Brodie and Tom Knight. There have been three occasions when two players have scored hat-tricks in the same match – Billy Halligan and Jack Needham in an 8–0 win over top-of-the-table Hull City in 1911–12; Billy Hartill (4) and Charlie Phillips in a 9–1 FA Cup victory against Wrexham in 1930–31; and Roy Swinbourne and Johnny Hancocks in the 9–1 win at Cardiff City in 1955–56. The greatest number of individuals to score hat-tricks in a single season occurred in 1958–59 when Bobby Mason, Peter Broadbent, Colin Booth, Norman Deeley and Micky Lill all achieved the feat. Two players have scored hat-tricks on their league début. Jesse Pye did so in a 6–1 win over Arsenal on the opening day of the 1946–47 season and Dennis Wilshaw against Newcastle United in March 1949 in a 3–0 home win. On 27 September 1992, Darren Roberts scored a televised hat-trick in a 4–0 win at Birmingham City in what was his first full game for the club. The fastest hat-trick by a Wolves player is eight minutes, achieved by Dennis Westcott against Liverpool on 7 December 1946. Steve Bull holds the record for the most hat-tricks in a season – 1988–89 – and he also holds the club record for the most in a career with 17.

**HAWKINS, GRAHAM** Tall, blond, central defender Graham Hawkins began his career in the First Division with Wolverhampton Wanderers and made his début against West Bromwich Albion in October 1964. He was never a regular at Molineux and after only 35 appearances in four seasons, he moved to Preston North End. Seen as a successor to Tony Singleton, he did not make too many appearances in his early days owing to his misfortune of being injured on his North End début. He was one of the club's youngest ever captains at 22, and went on to make 245 league appearances for the Deepdale club before joining neighbours Blackburn Rovers in June 1974. There he played 109 league games before moving to Port Vale where he ended his playing career. After a spell as assistant-manager at Shrewsbury Town, he was employed by Derek Dougan when the Irish international became chief executive at Molineux and helped the club regain their top-flight status as runners-up to

Queen's Park Rangers in 1982–83. He made some shrewd signings but after Wolves failed to win any of their first 16 games in the First Division and were relegated straight back, it came as no surprise that he was sacked.

**HAYWOOD, ADAM** Able to play in all of the forward positions, Adam Haywood joined Wolves from New Brompton where he appeared in a North v South England trial. He signed for Wolves in the summer of 1901 and scored the opening goal on his début in a 2–0 home win over Nottingham Forest in the first game of the 1901–02 season. He was the club's top scorer in 1902–03, with 11 goals in 24 games, and went on to find the net 28 times in 113 first-team outings before leaving to join West Bromwich Albion in May 1905. He later played for Blackpool before becoming player-coach at Crystal Palace.

**HEDLEY, GEORGE** George Hedley was a robust, aggressive player who began his career as an amateur in the Northern League before joining Sheffield United in May 1898. At the end of his first season with the Yorkshire club, Hedley won an FA Cup winners' medal when the Blades beat Derby County 4–1. Three years later he won his second FA Cup winners' medal when United beat Southampton, Hedley scoring the opening goal in a 2–1 win after the first game had been drawn. Hedley, who was capped against Ireland in March 1901, found that his career was threatened by torn heart muscles but despite medical advice he refused to give up the game and signed for Southampton. At The Dell, Hedley scored 30 goals in 70 games and helped the Saints win the Southern League Championship. In May 1906, Hedley joined Wolves and made his début in a 1–1 home draw against Hull City in the opening game of the 1906–07 season. Hedley ended the season with 11 goals in 37 games including a hat-trick in a 6–2 home win over Burslem Port Vale. The following season he was the club's top scorer with 16 goals in 33 games including one in the FA Cup final against Newcastle United when the Magpies were beaten 3–1 to give Hedley his third FA Cup winners' medal. After seven seasons at Molineux, during which time he had scored 74 goals in 214 league and cup games, he left to become manager of Bristol City for the two seasons immediately prior to the First World War.

**HIBBITT, KENNY** Goalscoring midfielder Kenny Hibbitt joined Wolves from Bradford Park Avenue in November 1968 and remained at Molineux for 16 years. He made his début as a substitute in a 1-0 home defeat by West Bromwich Albion in April 1969 but didn't appear again in the first team until September 1970, when he scored in a 2–2 draw at Chelsea. After that he established himself as a first-team regular and over the next 15 seasons missed very few games. Hibbitt was a great competitor and during his time at Molineux won two League Cup winners' medals in 1974 and 1980 and helped the club win promotion to the First Division in 1976–77 and 1982–83. His best season for Wolves in terms of goals scored were seasons 1974–75 and 1976–77 when he netted 17 league goals in each campaign. In 1974–75 he scored all four goals in a 4–2 home win over Newcastle United and a hat-trick in a 5–2 defeat of Luton Town. Hibbitt went on to score 114 goals in 574 first-team games before joining Coventry City in 1984, later moving to Bristol Rovers. Sadly his illustrious playing career came to an end when he broke his leg in Rovers' match against Sunderland in February 1988. Appointed as Gerry Francis's assistant, he helped the Twerton Park club to the Third Division Championship and to the final of the Leyland Daf Cup. He then became manager of Walsall and in 1992–93 led the Saddlers into the Third Division play-offs. He is now director of football with Cardiff City.

**HINTON, ALAN** Winger Alan Hinton began his Football League career with Wolverhampton Wanderers and played his first game for the club in January 1961 as Huddersfield Town drew 1–1 at Molineux in a third round FA Cup tie. It was in 1962–63 that Hinton had established himself as a first-team regular and he ended that campaign as the club's leading scorer with 19 goals in 38 league games including netting a hat-trick in a 5–0 win at Fulham. Having won England Youth and Under-23 honours, Hinton won the first of three full caps during his time at Molineux when he played against France in October 1962. He had scored 29 goals in 78 first team games for Wolves when in January 1964 he moved to Nottingham Forest. It was at the City Ground that he won his two other caps. He had scored 23 goals in 124 league and cup games for Forest when Brian Clough paid £30,000 to take the Wednesbury-born winger to Derby County. At the Baseball Ground, Hinton helped the Rams win the Second Division title and two League Championships and scored

*Kenny Hibbitt*

64 goals in 253 league appearances. After leaving league football he went to play in the NASL for a variety of teams – Dallas Tornado, Vancouver Whitecaps, Tulsa Roughnecks, Seattle Sounders and Tacoma Stars, for whom he continued to play in the Major Indoor Soccer League after the NASL folded.

**HODNETT, JOE** When Joe Hodnett arrived at Molineux from Willenhall in 1919 he found himself the club's fourth-choice centre-half. However, he worked his way through the ranks after making his début in a 4–2 home win over Hull City on 20 December 1919 and when Wolves played Spurs in the 1921 FA Cup final at Stamford Bridge, he found himself at the heart of the Molineux club's defence. That 1920–21 season was his most successful with Wolves, as he appeared in 34 games and struck up a fine understanding with half-backs Val Gregory and Alf Riley. He had appeared in 85 league and cup games, scoring five goals, when the Wolves board decided he was surplus to requirements and transferred him to Pontypridd in the summer of 1923. He later played for Chesterfield, Merthyr Town, Brentford and Gillingham before returning to the Midlands to play for Stafford Rangers. After that he continued to play non-league football in the area, turning out for Stourbridge, Halesowen, Dudley Town and Brierley Hill Alliance before hanging up his boots at the end of the 1935–36 season.

**HOLLINGWORTH, REG** Giant centre-half Reg Hollingworth played his early football with Nuffield Colliery before signing amateur forms with his local club Mansfield Town. They wanted to sign Hollingworth on professional terms but could not afford to pay him and he ended up at Molineux after a series of impressive performances for the Stags. He played his first game for Wolves on 10 November 1928 in a 2–0 win at West Bromwich Albion and after a couple of seasons gained a regular place on the side. He won a Second Division Championship medal in 1931–32, though a knee injury in the club's 2–0 win at home to Barnsley on 12 March 1932 not only forced him to miss the club's run-in to the title but also to pull out of an England international trial at Huddersfield when full honours looked likely. He had scored eight goals in 180 league and cup games when another knee injury forced him to retire prematurely from the game at the age of 27. The disappointed Hollingworth decided to join the Staffordshire Police Force, where he served as a constable for a good number of years. Sadly, he died of a heart attack while driving his car in Sparkbrook, Birmingham, in July 1969.

**HOLMES, MICKEY** Blackpool-born Mickey Holmes played his early football across the Pennines with Yeadon Colliery before joining Bradford City in the summer of 1983. However, he only managed five appearances as a substitute during his time at Valley Parade and after a spell on Burnley's books as a non-contract player, again failing to make a full league appearance, he joined Wolves in November 1985. After making his début in a 1–1 draw at Cardiff City, he scored the opening goal on his first appearance at Molineux as Wolves drew 2–2 with Wigan Athletic. He went on to score 13 goals in 104 games, winning Fourth Division Championship and Sherpa Van Trophy medals in 1987–88 before leaving at the end of the season to join Huddersfield Town. He later played for Cambridge United, Rochdale, Torquay United and Carlisle United.

**HOLSGROVE, JOHN** An England Youth international, John Holsgrove played as an amateur for both Spurs and Arsenal before joining Crystal Palace as an apprentice. The Southwark-born defender spent just one season in the Selhurst Park club's team, making 22 appearances before he joined Wolves on the recommendation of Ronnie Allen for a fee of £18,000. He made his début in a 3–0 home win over Bury on 25 September 1965 and over the next five seasons missed very few games, being an ever-present in 1967–68. That was the club's first season back in the top flight following their promotion the previous season when Holsgrove was one of Wolves' best players. At Molineux, Holsgrove struck up a fine understanding at the heart of the Wolves' defence, first with Dave Woodfield and then with Frank Munro, appearing in 97 consecutive games between 14 January 1967 and 1 February 1969. He lost his place to John McAlle at the start of the 1970–71 season, however, and after appearing in 202 league and cup games for the Molineux club, left to join Sheffield Wednesday. He spent four seasons in the Owls' first team playing in 104 league games before leaving to sign for Stockport County. Sadly, injury forced him to retire from league football after just half a season at Edgeley Park.

**HOME MATCHES** Wolves' best home wins are the 14–0 rout of Crosswell's Brewery in an FA Cup second-round tie on 13

November 1886 and a 10–1 defeat of Leicester City in a First Division game in 1937–38. The club also achieved double figures in a first round FA Cup replay in 1911–12, beating Watford 10–0 after the first match had been goalless! The club's worst home defeat is 7–1, a scoreline inflicted upon them by Arsenal in 1932–33.

**HOME SEASONS** Wolverhampton Wanderers have gone through a complete league season with an undefeated home record on just one occasion – 1923–24, when they won the Third Division (North) Championship. The club's highest number of home wins in a season is 18, achieved in seasons 1923–24 and 1988–89 when Wolves again won the Third Division Championship.

**HONOURS** The major honours achieved by the club are:

| | |
|---|---|
| First Division Championship | 1953–54  1957–58  1958–59 |
| Second Division Championship | 1931–32  1976–77 |
| Third Division Championship | 1923–24  1988–89 |
| Fourth Division Championship | 1987–88 |
| FA Cup Winners | 1893  1908  1949  1960 |
| League Cup Winners | 1974  1980 |
| FA Charity Shield | 1950*  1955*  1960  1961* |
| Texaco Cup Winners | 1971 |
| Sherpa Van Trophy Winners | 1988 |

* shared

**HOOPER, HARRY** Harry Hooper began his Football League career with West Ham United and whilst at Upton Park the speedy winger played six times for England 'B', twice for England Under-23s and also for the Football League XI. Though he was selected for the full England squad, he never played a full international whilst with the Hammers. During his six seasons with West Ham, he scored 44 goals in 130 games, with 1955–56 his best season in terms of goals scored – he netted 16 in 36 games including a hat-trick in a 6–1 win over Doncaster Rovers. In March 1956, Wolverhampton Wanderers paid £25,000 for his services and he scored on his début in a 5–1 home win over Manchester City on the opening day of the 1956–57 season. Hooper was in fact the club's top scorer with 19 goals in 39 games including a hat-trick in a 4–3 win over Preston North End as Wolves finished sixth in the First Division. However, in December

1957, Hooper left Molineux and joined Birmingham City where in 105 league games he scored 34 goals. In 1960 he moved again – this time to play for his home-town club Sunderland. He ended his career at Roker Park, where he scored 16 goals in 65 games.

**HORNE, DES** Johannesburg-born winger Des Horne was one of a number of players who came to Molineux from South Africa in the 1950s, hoping to make the grade in the Football League. He was one of the few who succeeded but though he signed professional forms in December 1956, he had to wait until the opening day of the 1958–59 season before making his début because of Jimmy Mullen's fine form. He had an outstanding first game for the club, laying on goals for Mason and Broadbent in a 5–1 home win over Nottingham Forest. Though Wolves retained the League Championship, Horne only appeared in eight games and had to wait until the following season before establishing himself in the first team. He won an FA Cup winners' medal in 1960, but after scoring 18 goals in 52 games, he was transferred to Blackpool in March 1961. At Bloomfield Road he helped the Seasiders to a League Cup semi-final but much of his time with the Lancashire club was spent in trying to avoid relegation from the top flight. He had scored 21 goals in 137 games when he left the Seasiders and returned to his native South Africa.

**HOSKINS, ALBERT** After failing to make the grade as a player at Molineux, Albert Hoskins worked his way up from office boy to become club secretary. For a good number of years he was assistant to Jack Addenbrooke before taking over from him in May 1924. Hoskins efficiently combined his duties as the club secretary with those of organising the playing side. In 1924–25, his first season in charge, the club finished a very creditable sixth in the Second Division and fourth the following term. Hoskins, however, surprisingly left the club in March 1926 (when Fred Scotchbrook took over) to join Gillingham as secretary-manager. After a spell at Torquay United, he worked as a trainer, coach and scout for a number of non-league clubs, but on the outbreak of war in 1939 he left the game.

**HUGHES, EMLYN** The son of a Great Britain Rugby League international, Emlyn Hughes first played for Blackpool before Liverpool manager Bill Shankly signed the 19-year-old for £65,000 in February 1967. At the press conference, Shanks said that one day the young man would captain England. He was right, and if any player epitomised the Liverpool style of play in the 1970s, it was 'Crazy Horse'. Hughes went on to win 59 caps at Anfield to become the club's most capped England player. Footballer of the Year in 1977, Hughes won two European Cup winners' medals, two UEFA Cup medals, four League Championship medals and an FA Cup winners' medal. With his Liverpool career drawing to a close, Hughes, who had made 657 first-team appearances for the Reds, joined Wolves for a fee of £90,000 in August 1979. Whilst with the Molineux club he added three more international caps to his collection, and after starring in the heart of the Wolves' defence in 1979–80 when the club finished sixth in the First Division, he captained the club to League Cup success over Nottingham Forest at Wembley. Hughes' signing was only ever going to be short-term and in September 1981, after appearing in 76 games, he joined Rotherham United as player-manager. He later played for Hull City and Swansea before hanging up his boots. Awarded the OBE for his services to football, he has since worked in television, notably as a team captain on *A Question of Sport*.

**HUMPHREY, JOHN** Paddington-born full-back John Humphrey joined Wolves as an apprentice in February 1979 and, though he made his début in a 3–0 win at Southampton in April 1980, it was midway through the 1981–82 season before he established himself on the side. Sadly the Molineux club were relegated to the Second Division at the end of that campaign but when they returned to the top flight at the first time of asking as runners-up to Queen's Park Rangers, Humphrey was ever-present. Unbelievably, Wolves lost their First Division status after just one season and then finished bottom of Division Two in 1984–85. Humphrey, who had played all his football in the top two divisions, left Molineux after making 164 first-team appearances to join Charlton Athletic. In his first season with the London club, he helped them win promotion to the First Division and made 231 appearances before joining Crystal Palace for a fee of £400,000. At the end of his first season with the Eagles, he helped them win the Zenith Data Systems Cup and in 1993–94 was instrumental in Palace winning the First Division Championship. He had appeared in 203 games for the Selhurst Park club when he returned to Charlton on a free transfer. He took his total of appearances for the Addicks to 267 before joining Gillingham and subsequently Brighton, where he ended his league career before playing for Chesham United in the Ryman's Isthmian League.

**HUNDRED GOALS** Wolves have scored more than 100 league goals in a season on five occasions. Their highest total is 115 goals scored in 1931–32 when they won the Second Division. They scored 103 goals in 1957–58 and 110 goals in 1958–59, winning the League Championship on both occasions. The Molineux club also scored 106 goals in 1959–60 and 103 goals in 1960–61 when they finished second and third in Division One respectively.

**HUNT, ERNIE** Ernie Hunt was working for British Rail when Swindon Town manager Bert Head signed him as an amateur in 1957. With the Wiltshire club, Hunt, whose real first name is Roger, won three England Under-23 caps and scored 82 goals in 214 league games before signing for Wolves in September 1965. He should have made his début at Southampton but he decided that he wasn't fully match fit and watched from the stands as the Saints won 9–3! He did make his début in the next match, however, creating goals for Knowles, Wagstaffe and Wharton in a 3–0 home win over Bury. The following season he helped Wolves win promotion to the First Division, top-scoring with 20 goals in 37 games including a hat-trick in a 4–0 win at Northampton Town. Hunt, who had an excellent scoring record for a midfielder, had found the net 35 times in 82 outings for Wolves before joining Everton for £80,000. Unable to settle at Goodison Park, he signed for Coventry City where he teamed up with a Wolves player of the future in Willie Carr. The two of them perfected the infamous 'donkey-kick' which resulted in a spectacular goal on *Match of the Day*. Hunt scored 45 goals in 146 league games for the Sky Blues before a loan spell with Doncaster Rovers. He ended his career with Bristol City.

**HUNT, REVEREND KENNETH** The Reverend Kenneth Hunt, who remained an amateur throughout his playing days, gained a soccer Blue at Oxford University and played for the great amateur side Corinthians. As well as playing for Wolves, he helped a number of other sides including Crystal Palace, Leyton and Oxford City. He gained 20 England amateur caps and appeared twice for the full international side. Hunt appeared for Wolves in 61 games between

1906 and 1920, scoring two goals, one of them in the 3–1 win over Newcastle United in the 1908 FA Cup final. That same year he won an Olympic gold medal with the Great Britain soccer team. He was an FA Council member for a number of years before ill health forced his retirement.

# I

**INTERNATIONAL MATCHES** There have been four international matches played at Molineux: the first, on 7 March 1891, saw England, with Wolves players Billy Rose and Jack Brodie on their side, beat Ireland 6–1. England met Ireland again at Molineux on 14 February 1903, a game in which Wolves' keeper Tom Baddeley kept a clean sheet, and England won 4–0. The third international match to be played at Molineux was on 5 February 1936 when England – without any Wolves players on their side – lost 2–1 to Wales! The last international match played on the Wolves' ground was on 5 December 1956 when England, captained by Billy Wright, beat Denmark 5–2 in a World Cup qualifier.

**INTERNATIONAL PLAYERS** Wanderers' most capped player (i.e.:caps gained while players were registered with the club) is Billy Wright with 105 caps. The first Wolverhampton Wanderers player to be capped was Charlie Mason, who played for England v Ireland on 5 February 1887, a game which England won 7–0. The following is a complete list of players who have gained full international honours for England, Scotland, Wales, Northern Ireland or the Republic of Ireland:

| England | No. of Caps | Scotland | No. of Caps |
|---|---|---|---|
| Harry Allen | 5 | Hugh Curran | 5 |
| Tom Baddeley | 5 | Andy Gray | 13 |
| Dicky Baugh Snr | 2 | Jim McCalliog | 1 |
| Billy Beats | 2 | Frank Munro | 9 |
| Peter Broadbent | 7 | **Northern Ireland** | |
| Jack Brodie | 3 | Jim Brown | 1 |
| Steve Bull | 13 | Robbie Dennison | 18 |
| Eddie Clamp | 4 | Derek Dougan | 26 |
| Chris Crowe | 1 | Billy Halligan | 1 |
| Stan Cullis | 12 | Danny Hegan | 6 |
| Norman Deeley | 2 | Bertie Lutton | 2 |
| Albert Fletcher | 2 | Peter McParland | 1 |
| Ron Flowers | 49 | David Martin | 2 |
| Tom Galley | 2 | Sammy Smyth | 8 |
| Johnny Hancocks | 3 | **Wales** | |
| Alan Hinton | 1 | George Berry | 4 |
| Emlyn Hughes | 3 | Jack Bowdler | 2 |
| Revd Kenneth Hunt | 2 | Josiah Davies | 2 |
| George Kinsey | 2 | Ryan Green | 2 |
| Arthur Lowder | 1 | Bryn Jones | 10 |
| Charlie Mason | 3 | Albert Lumberg | 1 |
| Bill Morris | 3 | Jack Mathais | 1 |
| Jimmy Mullen | 12 | Teddy Peers | 8 |
| Jesse Pye | 1 | Charlie Phillips | 10 |
| John Richards | 1 | Dai Richards | 11 |
| Billy Rose | 4 | Dick Richards | 5 |
| Bill Slater | 12 | Adrian Williams | 2 |
| Tom Smalley | 1 | Eric Young | 1 |
| Bobby Thomson | 8 | **Republic of Ireland** | |
| Dick Topham | 1 | Maurice Daly | 2 |
| Bert Williams | 24 | David Jordan | 2 |
| Dennis Wilshaw | 12 | Robbie Keane | 3 |
| Harry Wood | 3 | Mick Kearns | 2 |
| Billy Wright | 105 | David Kelly | 4 |
| | | Phil Kelly | 5 |

# J

**JOBEY, GEORGE** As a player, George Jobey began his Football League career with Newcastle United where he won a League Championship medal in 1908–09 and an FA Cup runners-up medal in 1911. In May 1913 he joined Woolwich Arsenal for a fee of £500 and scored the Gunners' first goal at their new Highbury ground. After just one season he joined Bradford and then appeared for Hamilton Academicals during the First World War. When the hostilities were over, he played for Leicester City and Northampton Town before retiring in September 1922 to become manager of Wolverhampton Wanderers. In his first season with the club, they finished bottom of the Second Division with only 27 points, having scored just 42 goals. Jobey then worked miracles to turn the Molineux club's fortunes around and they won the Third Division (North) Championship by one point from Rochdale. Jobey was renowned for his disciplinarian approach and often frightened his players so much that they became nervous wrecks if they displeased him. After his surprise departure from Molineux at the end of that championship-winning season, he ran a hotel for a year until Derby County enticed him back into the game as their manager in the summer of 1925. He really made a name for himself at the Baseball Ground, leading the Rams back into the First Division at the end of his first season with the club. He signed three of County's greatest-ever players in Jack Barker, Jack Bowers and Sammy Crooks and, in 1929–30 and 1935–36, he led the club to the runners-up spot in the First Division. In May 1941, Jobey was suspended for life when it was discovered that the Derby manager had been paying illegal bonuses to his players since being appointed in 1925. The suspension was lifted in 1945 but he didn't return to the game until 1952 when he became manager of Mansfield Town.

**JONES, BRYN** Inside-forward Bryn Jones worked down the pit whilst playing for his home-town club Merthyr Amateurs and then Plymouth United in the South Wales District League. After being rejected by Southend United, he played for Glenavon in the Irish League before returning to Wales to play for Aberaman in the summer of 1933. However, he was soon on his way to Molineux for a fee of £1,500 and made his début against Everton at Goodison Park in a match Wolves won 2–1. In his second season with the club he won the first of 17 Welsh caps when he played against Northern Ireland. Jones stayed at Molineux for five seasons, scoring 57 goals in 177 games including a hat-trick in a 4–2 home win over Preston North End on 20 April 1936. His best season in terms of goals scored was 1937–38 when he netted 15 in 36 league games, but at the end of that campaign he left to join Arsenal for a record fee of £14,000. He scored Arsenal's first goal on his début in a 2–0 home win over Portsmouth and followed this by scoring twice in the next three league games. However, war was just around the corner and Jones was posted to Italy and North Africa while serving with the Royal Artillery. On his return to Highbury, he helped the Gunners win the League Championship in 1947–48. His Arsenal career finished while on the summer tour of Brazil in 1949 but shortly after becoming Norwich City's player-coach, he was recommended, on doctor's advice, to retire from the game.

**JONES, JACK** A marvellous servant to Wolverhampton Wanderers, he joined the club from local side Lanesfield FC in 1900 and made his first-team début in a 2–0 home win over Nottingham Forest on the opening day of the 1901–02 season. Jones was the club's only ever-present that season, a feat he achieved in the following two seasons, going on to make 109 consecutive league appearances. He was ever-present again in seasons 1905–06 and 1906–07, this time appearing in 102 consecutive league games. He won an FA Cup winners' medal in 1908 as Wolves beat Newcastle United 3–1 at Crystal Palace. Jones had played in 336 league and cup games for Wolves when, after hanging up his boots, he became the club's trainer. A well known figure around Molineux, he could often be seen smoking his pipe with his FA Cup winners' medal proudly hanging from his watch chain!

**JUBILEE FUND** The League Benevolent Fund was launched in 1938,

50 years after the start of the Football League, to benefit players who had fallen on hard times. It was decided that the best way to raise funds was for sides to play local derby games with no account being taken of league status. At the start of the 1938–39 season, Wolves beat Stoke City 4–3 at Molineux with goals from Reg Kirkham (2), Dickie Dorsett and Teddy MacGuire. In the return fixture at the start of the following season, Wolves beat Stoke at the Victoria Ground 4–2 with Dickie Dorsett scoring a hat-trick.

**KAY, ALBERT** Sheffield-born defender Albert Kay played his early football with Tinsley FC before later playing for Birmingham and then Willenhall, from whom he joined Wolves in the summer of 1921. He made his first-team début in September 1922 in a 1–1 draw at Derby County and over the next ten seasons went on to appear in 295 games, mainly at wing-half or full-back. He showed his versatility by taking over the goalkeeper's jersey on a number of occasions and, though he once saved a penalty in a Central League match, he did concede four second-half goals in a 7–3 defeat at West Bromwich Albion in December 1929 after he had replaced the injured Billy Walker. He won a Third Divison (North) Championship medal in 1923–24 and played his part in helping the club win the Second Division Championship in 1931–32. Sadly, injury forced his retirement at the end of that season before he got the chance to sample First Division football.

**KEANE, ROBBIE** Republic of Ireland international Robbie Keane made his début for Wolves in the opening game of the 1997–98 season, scoring both goals in a 2–0 win at Norwich City, thus becoming the first Wolves player to score two goals on his début since Ted Farmer in 1960. He hit another 'double' in only his fourth league game as Wolves beat Bury at Molineux 4–2. The Dublin-born youngster became the Republic's second youngest full international ever, when he came on as a substitute and played most of the second-half against Czechoslovakia. Robbie Keane was certainly the find of the 1997–98 season and fully deserved his selection in the PFA divisional team.

**KELLY, DAVID** A Republic of Ireland international who scored a hat-trick on his full début against Israel in November 1987, David Kelly began his league career with Walsall after joining them from non-league Alvechurch. He proved himself to be a prolific scorer with the Saddlers, netting 80 goals in 190 first-team games before leaving to join West Ham United in the summer of 1988 for a fee of £600,000. Unable to settle at Upton Park, he was allowed to join Leicester City for £300,000. He scored 25 goals in 75 games for the Foxes before signing for promotion-chasing Newcastle United in December 1991 for £250,000. After helping the Magpies win the First Division Championship, he joined Wolverhampton Wanderers in the summer of 1993 for £750,000. He played his first game for the Molineux club in a 3–0 home win over Bristol City on the opening day of the 1993–94 season and scored 11 goals in 36 league games, playing alongside Steve Bull. He continued to find the net on a regular basis the following season, scoring a hat-trick in a 5–1 win at Bristol City. He had scored 36 goals in 103 games when he joined Sunderland for £1 million in September 1995. Damaged ankle ligaments restricted his appearances for the Wearsiders but he became the club's record signing after £100,000 – with an extra payment to Wolves if Sunderland reached the Premiership – was made. He played in 40 games for the north-east club before moving to Tranmere Rovers in the summer of 1997.

**KENDALL, MARK** A Welsh Youth international goalkeeper, Mark Kendall made his only appearance for his country at Under-21 level when he played against Scotland in February 1978, some nine months before he made his Football League début for Tottenham Hotspur. Despite stiff competition from Barry Daines and Milija Aleksic, Kendall appeared in 36 league and cup games before joining Newport County for an initial loan period. He went on to give the Somerton Park club excellent service, playing 319 first-team games over six years. Due to Newport's financial situation growing ever worse, however, he moved to Wolves in December 1986. He made his début on New Year's Day in a 3–0 home defeat by Peterborough United before going on to appear in 106 consecutive league games. In his first season with the club, Wolves reached the play-offs but in 1987–88 they won both the Fourth Division Championship and the Sherpa Van Trophy. Throughout that campaign, Kendall was instrumental in the club's success, keeping 28 clean sheets in 61 games. In 1988–89 Kendall kept 13 clean sheets in 36 league games as Wolves won the Third Division Championship. He stayed at

Molineux for three and a half seasons and appeared in 177 league and cup games before being released in the summer of 1990. He then joined Swansea City and, although he spent much of his time at the Vetch Field in the reserves, he did help them win the Welsh Cup.

**KINDON, STEVE** After starring in Burnley's FA Youth Cup run of 1967–68, Steve Kindon became the first member of the Clarets' victorious Youth Cup side to establish himself in the First Division. He scored on his Turf Moor début in a 3–1 win over West Ham United, and after winning Youth international honours, he was ever-present in Burnley's First Division side of 1969–70, top-scoring with 17 goals. After the Lancashire club were relegated in 1971, Kindon was unable to sustain the form that his speed and talent warranted. He joined Wolverhampton Wanderers for a fee of £100,000 in the summer of 1972 and scored on his début in a 2–1 defeat at Newcastle United on the opening day of the 1972–73 season. However, it took him a while to settle down in the Midlands and he only appeared briefly in the club's successful League Cup run in 1973–74, missing out on the final when Wolves beat Manchester City 2–1. Though the club were relegated at the end of the 1975–76 season, they bounced straight back as Second Division Champions the following season with Kindon playing his part. He had scored 31 goals in 167 games for Wolves when he returned to Burnley in November 1977 for £80,000. He spent two more seasons at Turf Moor taking his tally of goals to 58 in 225 games before joining Huddersfield Town where a knee injury ended his career.

**KINSEY, GEORGE** Though he only spent three seasons playing for Wolves, George Kinsey won an FA Cup winners' medal in 1893 as the Molineux club beat Everton 1–0 at Fallowfield, and he played twice for England. The tough-tackling full-back played his early football with Burton Crusaders, Burton Swifts and Mitchell St George's before arriving at Molineux in the summer of 1891. After playing in a 5–2 defeat at Sunderland on the opening day of the 1891–92 season, Kinsey went on to score three goals in 83 league and cup games before being transferred to Aston Villa in June 1894. After failing to settle at Villa Park, he joined Derby County where he was ever-present as the Rams played their first season of league football at the Baseball Ground. In 1895–96 he helped Derby to the runners-up spot in Division One and to the FA Cup semi-finals where, despite Kinsey having an outstanding game, his old club beat the Rams 2–1. He won another two caps for England before leaving to play for Notts County for a short spell. After that, he helped to establish Bristol Rovers in the Southern League.

**KIRKHAM, JOHN** England Youth international John Kirkham made his début for Wolves in a 3–2 home win over Manchester United in October 1959, though over the next two seasons he only made 11 first-team appearances. It was 1961-62 before he established himself as a first-team regular for the Molineux club, a campaign in which he made 29 appearances. He opened his goalscoring account with both goals in the 2–1 home win over Nottingham Forest and followed it up with another in a 2–0 win at Old Trafford against Manchester United in the next game. He had scored 15 goals in 112 games for Wolves when he lost his place to Freddie Goodwin and moved on to Peterborough United. After making 46 league appearances for the 'Posh', he joined Exeter City where he played in 34 games before hanging up his boots.

**KNOWLES, PETER** Peter Knowles joined Wolves' nursery side Wath Wanderers in 1961 and turned professional in October 1962. Twelve months later he made his league début in a 1–0 win at Leicester City and the following season established himself as a first-team regular. Sadly the club were relegated that season, but in 1965–66 Knowles was in fine form and scored 21 goals in 34 games including hat-tricks against Carlisle United (Home 3–0) and Derby County (Home 4–0). When Wolves won promotion to the First Division in 1966–67, Knowles was hampered by injuries but still contributed eight goals in 21 games. Knowles, who was capped four times by England at Under-23 level, looked likely to win full international honours but in 1970, after scoring 64 goals in 191 games, he turned his back on the game and became a Jehovah's Witness. Knowles was only 24 and his sudden departure from football was a great shock to Wolves fans.

*Peter Knowles*

# L

**LARGEST CROWD** It was on 11 February 1939 that Molineux housed its largest crowd. The occasion was the FA Cup fifth round match against Liverpool. A staggering crowd of 61,315 saw Wolves win 4–0 with goals from Burton, Dorsett, McIntosh and Westcott. The club went on to reach that season's final at Wembley but went down 4–1 to Portsmouth.

**LATE FINISHES** Wolves' final match of the season against Liverpool at Molineux on 31 May 1947 is the latest date for the finish of any Wanderers' season. For the record, the visitors won 2–1 in front of 50,765 spectators. During the Second World War many curious things occurred, among them the continuance of the 1941–42 season into June. Thus, Wolves' last competitive match in that campaign was on 6 June, when a goal from Jimmy Mullen gave them a 1–1 draw at Brentford.

**LEAGUE GOALS – CAREER HIGHEST** Steve Bull holds the Molineux record for the most league goals with a career total of 246 goals between 1986–87 and 1997–98.

**LEAGUE GOALS – LEAST CONCEDED** During the 1923–24 season, Wolves conceded just 27 goals in 42 games when winning the Third Division (North) Championship.

**LEAGUE GOALS – MOST INDIVIDUAL** Dennis Westcott holds the Wolves record for the most league goals in a season with 38 scored in the First Division during the 1946–47 season.

**LEAGUE GOALS – MOST SCORED** Wolves' highest goals tally in the Football League was during the club's Second Division

Championship-winning season of 1931–32 when they scored 115 goals.

**LEAGUE VICTORY – HIGHEST** Wolves' best league victory is the 10–1 win over Leicester City at Molineux on 15 April 1938. Both Dickie Dorsett and Dennis Westcott netted four goals apiece, with one each from Bryn Jones and Teddy Macguire.

**LEADING GOALSCORERS** Wolverhampton Wanderers have provided the Football League's divisional leading goalscorer on three occasions:

| | | | |
|---|---|---|---|
| 1946–47 | Dennis Westcott | Division One | 38 goals |
| 1987–88 | Steve Bull | Division Four | 34 goals |
| 1988–89 | Steve Bull | Division Three | 37 goals |

**LEE, COLIN** Colin Lee joined Bristol City as a central striker, but opportunities in that position were limited at Ashton Gate, so he switched to full-back and in that role was loaned out to Hereford and Torquay before joining the Devon club on a permanent basis. He reverted to striker at Plainmoor and caught the eye of Spurs boss Keith Burkinshaw who signed him for £60,000 in November 1977. He made a remarkable début for the White Hart Lane club, scoring four goals in a 9–0 defeat of Bristol Rovers. He went on to score 31 goals in 94 games before joining Chelsea for £200,000. He spent seven years with the West London club, winning a Second Division Championship medal and a Full Members' Cup medal. In 1987 he joined Brentford as player/youth development officer before moving to Watford to be in charge of their youth team. In 1991 he joined Reading as assistant-manager under Mark McGhee and three years later followed him to Leicester City as his assistant. When McGhee was appointed Wolves manager, Lee moved to Molineux as his number two and in November 1998 took over as caretaker-boss and guided the club to a 6–1 win at Bristol City, their best away win for 22 years. His successful unbeaten run as caretaker made him the board's clear choice to succeed McGhee, and he was installed in the Molineux hot seat until the end of the 1998–99 season.

**LEES, HARRY** Harry Lees was a clever inside-left who played his early football as an amateur with Notts County before moving to

Welsh football and Ebbw Vale. He joined Wolves for a fee of £50 in February 1923 and moved straight into the side for the game at Bradford City which Wolves drew 1–1. In 1923–24, his first full season with the club, he helped Wolves win the Third Division (North) Championship, top–scoring with 21 goals. His total included hat–tricks in the 5–1 home win over New Brighton and the 3–0 defeat of Wrexham, also at Molineux. He went on to score 43 goals in 129 first-team outings before leaving to join Darlington at the end of the 1927–28 season. After netting five goals in 26 games for the Quakers, he entered non-league football with Shrewsbury Town, later playing for Stourbridge and Leamington Town.

**LITTLE, BRIAN** Brian Little began his career with Aston Villa where he played an important part in the club's FA Youth Cup success. He went on to win League Cup winners' medals in 1975 and 1977, scoring two of Villa's goals in the 3–2 win over Everton in the third match of that final at Old Trafford. He was the Second Division's leading scorer in 1974–75 with 20 goals including a hat-trick in a 5–0 win over Oldham Athletic. At the end of that season, he won his only England cap when he came on as a substitute for the final ten minutes of the match against Wales at Wembley. Sadly he was forced to give up the game on medical grounds. He had a spell working in the club's promotion department before moving to Molineux as first-team coach. He then replaced Sammy Chapman as manager. He was replaced by Graham Turner a few weeks later and has since managed a number of clubs including Darlington, Leicester City and Aston Villa, whom he led to League Cup success. He is now in charge of Stoke City.

**LOS ANGELES WOLVES** Playing under the name of Los Angeles Wolves, the Molineux club won the prestigious International Soccer Tournament in America in 1966–67. They beat sides from Brazil, Holland, Italy and Uruguay to reach the final where they achieved victory over Aberdeen. The score was 6–5, with David Burnside scoring a hat-trick.

**LOWDER, ARTHUR** Left-half Arthur Lowder had the distinction of playing in the club's first-ever FA Cup tie against Long Eaton Rangers in 1883 and in the first Football League game against Aston Villa in 1888. In February 1889, Lowder was capped by England and starred in a 4–1 win over Wales at Stoke's Victoria Ground. A month later he was a member of the Wolves' side that lost to Preston North End in that season's FA Cup final, as the Deepdale side went on to the first-ever league and cup 'double'. Lowder, who had played in 71 games for Wolves, was forced to retire through injury in 1901. In later years he worked in Europe as a coach in France, Germany and Norway before returning to these shores in 1924.

**LOWEST** The lowest number of goals scored by Wolverhampton Wanderers in a single Football League season is 27 in 1983–84. The club's lowest points total in the Football League occurred in 1905–06 when Wolves gained just 23 points and were relegated from the First Division.

**LOWTON, WILF** Wilf Lowton began his Football League career with his home-town club Exeter City and had made 75 appearances for the Grecians when he joined Wolverhampton Wanderers for £1,400 in 1929. He made his début in a 4–2 home defeat by West Bromwich Albion on the opening day of the 1929–30 season. He missed just two games in that campaign and was a virtual ever-present over the next six seasons, playing in 209 first-team games. When Wolves won the Second Division Championship in 1931–32, Lowton was the captain and scored from the penalty spot nine times as the Molineux club finished two points ahead of runners-up Leeds United. In fact, Lowton was particularly dangerous from dead-ball situations and scored 29 goals for the club. He left Molineux midway through the 1934–35 season to return to Exeter City and appeared in a further 18 league games before becoming the Devon club's assistant-trainer.

# M

**MALPASS, BILLY** Half-back Billy Malpass joined Wolverhampton
Wanderers from Wednesbury Old Athletic in the summer of 1891
and played his first game for the club on 19 September 1891 in a 4–3
defeat at West Bromwich Albion. He established himself in the
club's defence in 1892–93 and, at the end of the season, was one of
Wolves' most outstanding players beating Everton 1–0 to win the FA
Cup final at Fallowfield. When Wolves reached the FA Cup final
again in 1896, Malpass was captain of the side, though this time they
were beaten 2–1 by Sheffield Wednesday. It was during this 1895–96
season that Malpass, along with Tommy Dunn and Alf Griffin, was
suspended for reportedly not trying on the field of play! The
following season he represented the Football League against the
Irish League in Belfast. He went on to play in 155 League and Cup
games before a persistent knee injury forced his retirement.

**MANAGERS** This is the complete list of Wolves' full-time managers
with their terms of office:

| | | | |
|---|---|---|---|
| Jack Addenbrooke | 1885–22 | John Barnwell | 1978–81 |
| George Jobey | 1922–24 | Ian Greaves | 1982 |
| Albert Hoskins | 1924–26 | Graham Hawkins | 1982–84 |
| Fred Scotchbrook | 1926–27 | Tommy Docherty | 1984–85 |
| Major Frank Buckley | 1927–44 | Sammy Chapman | 1985 |
| Ted Vizard | 1944–48 | Bill McGarry | 1985 |
| Stan Cullis | 1948–64 | Sammy Chapman | 1985–86 |
| Andy Beattie | 1964–65 | Brian Little | 1986 |
| Ronnie Allen | 1965–68 | Graham Turner | 1986–94 |
| Bill McGarry | 1968–76 | Graham Taylor | 1994–95 |
| Sammy Chung | 1976–78 | Mark McGhee | 1995–98 |
| | | Colin Lee | 1998– |

**MARATHON MATCHES** Wolverhampton Wanderers have been involved in a number of cup games that have gone to three matches. These are: Derby County (FA Cup second round 1903–04); Sunderland (FA Cup sixth round 1936–37); Aston Villa (FA Cup fifth round 1964–65); Grimsby Town (League Cup fifth round 1979–80); Coventry City (FA Cup third round 1983–84) and Chorley (FA Cup first round 1986–87). In their pre-league days, Wolves were involved in four matches against Aston Villa in a third-round tie in 1886–87. After three drawn games, Villa won 2–0.

**MARSHALL, GEORGE** Left-back George Marshall had trials with Portsmouth in 1913–14 but as nothing came of these he joined Southend United at the end of the season. War interrupted his career, however, and in August 1919, when league football resumed, Marshall joined Wolverhampton Wanderers. After a season in the Molineux club's reserve side, he made his first-team début in a 2–0 defeat at Fulham on the opening day of the 1920–21 season. By the end of that campaign, in which the Geordie-born defender missed only four games, he won an FA Cup runners-up medal after Wolves lost to Spurs in the final at Stamford Bridge. After losing his place to Harry Shaw, Marshall, who had appeared in 111 games, was transferred to Walsall in February 1924. His stay at Fellows Park was short and he moved to Reading before returning to the Midlands and ending his career with Darlaston.

**MARKSMEN – LEAGUE** Wolves' top league goalscorer is Steve Bull, who has struck 246 league goals during his 13 years at Molineux. Only 11 players have hit more than 100 league goals for the club:

| 1. | Steve Bull | 246 |
|---|---|---|
| 2. | Billy Hartill | 162 |
| 3. | Johnny Hancocks | 158 |
| 4. | Jimmy Murray | 155 |
| 5. | John Richards | 144 |
| 6. | Peter Broadbent | 127 |
| 7. | Harry Wood | 110 |
| 8. | Roy Swinbourne | 107 |
| 9. | Dennis Westcott | 105 |
| 10. | Dennis Wilshaw | 105 |
| 11. | Tom Phillipson | 104 |
| 12. | Jimmy Mullen | 98 |
| 13. | Andy Mutch | 96 |
| 14. | Derek Dougan | 95 |
| 15. | Jesse Pye | 90 |
| 16. | Kenny Hibbitt | 89 |
| 17. | Billy Wooldridge | 81 |
| 18. | Terry Wharton | 69 |
| 19. | Billy Beats | 67 |
| 20. | Norman Deeley | 66 |

**MARKSMEN – OVERALL** Fifteen players have hit a century of goals for Wolverhampton Wanderers. The club's top marksman is Steve Bull. The Century Club consists of:

| 1. | Steve Bull | 300 |
|---|---|---|
| 2. | John Richards | 194 |
| 3. | Billy Hartill | 170 |
| 4. | Johnny Hancocks | 168 |
| 5. | Jimmy Murray | 166 |
| 6. | Peter Broadbent | 145 |
| 7. | Harry Wood | 126 |
| 8. | Dennis Westcott | 124 |
| 9. | Derek Dougan | 123 |
| 10. | Kenny Hibbitt | 114 |
| 10. | Roy Swinbourne | 114 |
| 12. | Jimmy Mullen | 112 |
| 12. | Dennis Wilshaw | 112 |
| 14. | Tom Phillipson | 111 |
| 15. | Andy Mutch | 105 |

**MASON, BOBBY** Despite turning professional with the Molineux club in May 1953, inside-forward Bobby Mason had to wait until 5 November 1955 to make his first-team début in a 5–1 defeat at Luton Town. It was his only appearance that season and though he played in eight games the following campaign, it was 1957–58 before he became a first-team regular. That season saw Mason win the first of two League Championship medals as the Molineux club won the title for only the second time in their history. Mason scored a hat-trick in a 5–1 home win over Nottingham Forest on the opening day of the 1958–59 season and scored 13 goals in 34 games as Wolves won the League Championship for a second successive season. One disappointment for Mason during his time at Molineux came when he lost his place to young Barry Stobart for the 1960 FA Cup final against Blackburn Rovers, which Wolves won 3–0. Mason left Molineux in May 1962 after scoring 54 goals in 173 games to join non-league Chelmsford – but before long he was playing league football again, this time for Leyton Orient, where he later ended his career.

**MASON, CHARLIE** A founder member of the Wolverhampton Wanderers Football Club after leaving St Luke's School in 1877, full-back Charlie Mason played for the club for over 15 years. When he played for England against Ireland in 1887, he was the first Wolves player to appear in an international match. He played left-back for Wolves in their first appearance in an FA Cup final against Preston North End in 1889, having made his league début in the club's first game in the competition against Aston Villa. Mason appeared in 108 League and Cup games for Wolves and almost 300 in total when one includes games before the club acquired league status.

**MATCH OF THE DAY** Wolverhampton Wanderers' first appearance on BBC's *Match of the Day* was on 14 November 1964 when they beat Tottenham Hotspur at Molineux 3–1 with goals from Wharton, Crawford and Le Flem.

**McALLE, JOHN** Though he played his first game for Wolves in a 1–0 defeat at Chelsea in May 1968, McAlle had to wait over three seasons before becoming a regular in the Molineux club's side. Over the next nine seasons, the Liverpool-born defender missed very few

*John McAlle*

games and was ever-present in 1971–72 when Wolves finished ninth in Division One. That season was the only one in which he scored for the club, netting three goals, one in each leg of the UEFA Cup tie against Academica Coimbra and one in the League Cup against Manchester City. He won a League Cup winners' medal in 1974 but missed the 1980 final after breaking a leg in an FA Cup tie against Watford the previous month. He won a Second Division Championship medal in 1976 and enjoyed a deserved testimonial in 1978, but after the arrival of Emlyn Hughes he knew his days were numbered. After playing in 508 games he joined Sheffield United for £10,000 in the summer of 1981. Eight months later he moved to Derby County, where he ended his league career.

**McCALLIOG, JIM** When the Glasgow-born inside-forward joined Sheffield Wednesday from Chelsea for £37,500 in October 1965, he became the country's costliest teenager. By the end of that season he had helped the club reach the FA Cup final and scored the first goal in the 3–2 defeat by Everton. He was capped five times by Scotland and on his international début he scored in a 3–2 win against England at Wembley. He had scored 27 goals in 174 games for the Owls before he became unsettled and joined Wolves in the summer of 1969 for £70,000. He made his début in a 3–1 home win over Stoke City on the opening day of the 1969–70 season. One of only two ever-presents throughout that campaign, he went on to appear in 77 consecutive league games. He missed very few matches in his five seasons at Molineux and captained the team to the 1971–72 UEFA Cup final where he scored Wolves' goal in the 2–1 home-leg defeat by Tottenham Hotspur. He had scored 48 goals in 210 games when, after a short spell with Manchester United, he joined Southampton. The gifted ball-player scored two vital goals in the club's run to the FA Cup final in 1976 and was the architect of the goal that helped beat Manchester United. After leaving The Dell, he played in the United States for Chicago Sting before returning to England to become player-manager of Lincoln City. He later held a similar position with Runcorn before managing Halifax Town.

**McGARRY, BILL** Discovered by Port Vale in 1945, Bill McGarry moved to Huddersfield Town for a fee of £12,000 in March 1951. He soon established himself in the First Division and in 1954 he won the first of four England caps when he played in the World Cup finals in Switzerland. He was also capped for England 'B', played for the Football League and went on the FA's 1956 South African tour. He scored 26 goals in 381 League and Cup games for the Yorkshire club before becoming Bournemouth's first player-manager. From July 1963 he was the manager of Watford and in October 1964 he moved to Ipswich Town as manager. In 1967–68 he took the club to the Second Division Championship but in November 1968 he moved to take charge at Wolverhampton Wanderers. Renowned for his competitiveness as a player, he carried that approach into his managerial career at Molineux and led Wolves into Europe where they reached the final of the UEFA Cup. He also led them to success in the 1974 League Cup final before being sacked in the summer of 1976 after the club had been relegated. He later coached in Saudi Arabia and managed Newcastle United. There followed spells as Brighton scout, Power Dynamo (Zambia) coach, Zambian national team manager and a period as coach in South Africa before he spent 61 days in a second spell managing Wolves. Disillusioned, he quit the game before returning to South Africa to coach Bopnut-buswanana.

**McGHEE, MARK** Scottish international forward Mark McGhee made his mark with Morton where he scored 37 goals in 64 games before joining Newcastle United for a fee of £150,000. On leaving St James's Park he became an important member of Aberdeen's successful side of the early 1980s which won the European Cup Winners' Cup in 1983, beating Real Madrid in the final. He played in three Scottish Cup final victories for Aberdeen, along with two for Celtic whom he joined after a spell playing for SV Hamburg. On leaving Parkhead, he returned to Newcastle United for a second spell and took his tally of goals for the Magpies to 36 in 115 games before taking over as player-manager of Reading in May 1991. Though the team had a poor season in 1991–92, they came close to the play-offs in 1992–93 and the following season they won the Second Division Championship. After taking charge at Leicester City, McGhee defected to Wolves in December 1995, citing a lack of ambition at Filbert Street and the lure of the sleeping giants as his reasons for leaving. McGhee made an immediate impact with a run of seven games without defeat. At one stage it looked as if Wolves would reach the play-offs but a slump in fortunes meant they ended only two places above the relegation zone. In 1996–97 he led Wolves to third place in the First Division but they lost in the play-offs to Crystal Palace. In 1997–98 the club slipped to ninth place and in November 1998 he paid the price for the club's lack of success.

**McILMOYLE, HUGH** Much travelled centre-forward Hugh McIl-

*Hugh McIlmoyle*

moyle began his career with Port Glasgow before joining Leicester City in 1959 and playing in the FA Cup final of 1961. He then moved via Rotherham United to Carlisle United in March 1963 and was the Cumbrian side's leading marksman in their 1963–64 promotion success and FA Cup run. He joined Wolverhampton Wanderers in October 1964 for a fee of £30,000 and made his début in a 2–0 defeat at Fulham. Despite the club being relegated at the end of McIlmoyle's first season at Molineux, he had scored 14 goals in 32 games including a hat-trick in a 3–1 FA Cup fifth-round second-replay tie against Aston Villa. He continued to find the back of the net in 1965–66, scoring 17 goals in 44 league and cup games, but midway through the following season, when Wolves won promotion to the First Division, he was allowed to leave Molineux and join Bristol City. McIlmoyle, who had scored 45 goals in 105 games for Wolves, scored on his début for the Ashton Gate club but he never really settled. In September 1967 he rejoined Carlisle United for a cut-price £22,000. In 1968–69 he was ever-present and the top scorer, but after two years in his second spell at Brunton Park, he moved to the north-east to play for Middlesbrough. He later played for Preston North End and Morton before returning to Carlisle for a third spell, after which he ended his career. He had been a professional for 16 years during which time he had scored 153 league goals in 446 games for his seven clubs.

**McLEAN, GUS** One of the club's most versatile players, Gus McLean appeared in a variety of positions for Wolves during his nine years with the Molineux club. He signed for Wolves in November 1942 and appeared in 125 wartime games for the club before making his league début in a 6–1 home win over Arsenal on the opening day of the 1946–47 season. In that first league season after the Second World War, McLean missed just one match and played in more games than any other Wolves player. The following season he was chosen as a reserve for Wales against Scotland and though he continued to do sterling work for the Molineux club, he was forced to sit out the 1949 FA Cup final where Wolves beat Leicester City 3–1 because he had just undergone a cartilage operation. McLean appeared in 158 League and Cup games for Wolves, scoring two goals in a 3–1 win at Preston North End in 1947–48 and the only goal of the game at home to Portsmouth in 1949–50. He left Molineux at the end of the 1950–51 season to become player-manager of Aberystwyth Town and later first-team trainer at Bury. He was elected to take over from Brian Clough as manager of Hartlepool United and in 1967–68 steered them to their first-ever promotion. They were relegated the following season, however, and McLean was sacked.

**MERCANTILE CENTENARY FESTIVAL** The Mercantile Credit Centenary Festival took place at Wembley over the weekend of 16–17 April 1988. Qualification for the tournament was based on the number of league points won in the first 15 games after 1 November 1987. Eight clubs came from Division One, four from Division Two and two each from Divisions Three and Four. Wolves' games after 1 November brought nine wins, three draws and three defeats. Sadly, they went out of the competition to Everton – 3–2 on penalties – after having played out a 1–1 draw.

**MIDLAND VICTORY LEAGUE** The Midland Victory League came into being in March 1919. Wolves competed with Aston Villa, Derby County and West Bromwich Albion with the following results:

|  | Home | Away |
| --- | --- | --- |
| Aston Villa | 1–1 | 5–2 |
| Derby County | 1–1 | 0–4 |
| West Bromwich Albion | 1–1 | 1–0 |

**MILLER, JACK** Outside-left Jack Miller joined Wolves from his home-town club Hednesford Town in 1895, primarily as cover for the Scottish winger David Black. His first game for the club came in a 4–0 defeat at Bolton Wanderers in January 1896, though it was the following season when he established himself in the Wolves side. In fact, Miller missed very few games over the next seven seasons and in 1898–99 was the club's top scorer with 12 goals in 33 league appearances. The speedy winger went on to net 49 goals in 269 first-team games before signing for Stoke in the summer of 1905. For the Victoria Ground club, Miller scored five goals in 63 outings but left the Potters by mutual consent in 1907 to play non-league football.

**MITTON, JOHN** After playing as an amateur for Burnley, defender John Mitton 'guested' for Bury during the First World War before signing for Exeter City. After just 11 appearances for the Grecians in their first season of league football, he was transferred to Sunderland, the First Division side who paid £250 for his services. He scored seven goals in 82 games for the Wearsiders before Wolves signed him for £500 in the summer of 1924. He made his début in a

3–1 win at Port Vale on the opening day of the 1924–25 season as Wolves consolidated their position in the Second Division following promotion the previous season. He went on to play in 107 games for Wolves before being transferred to Southampton. He finally retired in 1930 after a short spell in Hampshire County soccer.

**MOLINEUX** Prior to Wolves' arrival at Molineux in 1889, the grounds had been established as a centre point for sport and leisure in the town of Wolverhampton for some time. There was a boating lake, croquet lawn and skating rink, and a number of athletic meetings and cycle races were held whilst the pitch was used for both cricket and football matches. By the time the Wanderers had appeared in the 1889 FA Cup final, the Molineux Grounds had been taken over by the Northampton Brewery and it was with them that the club had to negotiate to lease the ground. After lengthy discussions, it was decided that Wolves would only have to pay £50 a year rent to play at Molineux. The brewery then hurriedly converted the ground, building a 300-seater stand on Waterloo Road and erecting a shelter to cover a further 4,000 fans on what was an elevated cinder bank. Wolves' first game at Molineux as their home ground – for they had played Walsall Town in a Walsall Cup semi-final in 1886 – was a friendly against Aston Villa on 2 September 1889. However, only 3,000 fans turned up to see Wolves draw 1–1 because the game kicked off on a Monday at 5.30 p.m.! Five days later, Wolves played their first league match at Molineux, beating Notts County 2–0. In March 1891 the ground staged its first international match when England played Ireland and, in February 1892, the first of a number of FA Cup semi-finals was played at Molineux when Nottingham Forest played West Bromwich Albion. Despite housing another international and a number of FA Cup semi-finals, Molineux had fallen behind the other Midland club grounds – it didn't even have a main stand! In 1911, a curved roof was built over half the north end, an area of the ground that was soon to be known as the 'Cowshed'. In 1923, after the club had become a Limited Company, they purchased the freehold of Molineux from the Northampton Brewery for a fee of £5,607. The next development at Molineux was to transfer the terrace cover of 1889 from the Waterloo Road side of the ground to the Molineux Street side. Then the Scottish engineer Archibald Leitch built a new main stand on the Waterloo Road side of the ground at a cost of

£15,000 and this was opened in September 1925. During the next decade the 'Cowshed' was demolished and, following the club's promotion to the First Division in 1931–32, a new stand was built on Molineux Street. The stand's most prominent feature was its multi-span roof with seven gables, each painted old gold. This stand cost £20,000 to build and housed 3,450 seats and room for 4,500 standing on the paddock. In 1935 the South Bank, which was estimated to be able to hold 30,000 fans, had a pitched roof erected over the back of the terracing. After the Second World War came the advent of floodlighting and on 30 September 1953 Wolves played host to a South African XI in front of a Molineux crowd of 33,681. A series of floodlit friendlies followed, though in 1957 the ground's floodlights were replaced by a new set, the original ones having been too low. There was very little development at Molineux over the next couple of decades but in 1975, under the Safety of Sports Grounds Act, the ground's capacity was cut from 53,500 to 41,000. The club then bought and demolished over 70 late-Victorian terraced houses that stood behind the Molineux Street Stand before demolishing the stand itself. A new stand named after the club president John Ireland was built at a cost of £2 million and opened on 25 August 1979. The new stand, which had two tiers, could seat 9,230 spectators and housed 42 executive boxes. As a result, the club suffered four years of financial hardship with debts of around £2 million and was close to bankruptcy. No further developments were forthcoming and in 1985, after the fire at Bradford City's Valley Parade ground, the local authority closed down both the North Bank terracing and the Waterloo Road Stand. In the summer of 1986 the club went into receivership, but to make matters worse, safety officials even considered closing down the South Bank. It was in August 1986 that both the club and ground were saved by the Wolverhampton Metropolitan Council. The Council bought the 13 acres of Molineux and its training ground and social club for £1.1 million whilst the club's debt, which stood at £1.8 million, was paid off by a firm of developers called Gallaghers. They did so on the proviso that they would then have the right to build an Asda Superstore on wasteland behind the North Stand. However, the ground was still two-sided and it was only after the *Taylor Report* that the planning for an all-seater stadium went ahead. The arrival of Sir Jack Hayward, who paid £2.1 million to take over the club and ground, saw the start of the redevelopment work. In

October 1991, the North Bank was demolished and replaced by the Stan Cullis Stand at a cost of £2 million. Then the derelict Waterloo Road Stand which was replaced by the Billy Wright Stand, seating 8,659, was opened in August 1993. Later that year the South Bank was cleared and in its place was created the Jack Harris Stand, which was first used when the new Molineux was officially reopened on 7 December 1993 with a friendly against the Hungarian side Honved. Now housing an all-seater capacity of 28,525, Molineux is one of the finest football stadiums in the country.

**MORRIS, BILL** Though he was born only a short distance from West Bromwich Albion's ground at The Hawthorns, Bill Morris slipped through their net and, after playing for Handsworth Old Boys and Halesowen Town, signed for Wolves in the summer of 1933. Morris was a centre-forward when he joined Wolves and in fact his only two appearances for the first team in 1933–34 were both in that position. He was later converted to centre-half and was the club's first-choice pivot until the emergence of Stan Cullis, when he switched to right-back. His performances led to his winning three full caps for England, the first against Ireland in November 1938. At the end of that season he played in the FA Cup final against Portsmouth but then, of course, his career was interrupted by the Second World War. He appeared in 65 wartime games before playing in the first 10 games of the 1946–47 league campaign. Morris had appeared in 197 League and Cup games for Wolves when he left to play for Dudley Town in the Birmingham Combination.

**MOST MATCHES** Wolverhampton Wanderers played their greatest number of matches in season 1987–88, when they played 61. This comprised 46 league games, three FA Cup games, four Football League Cup games and eight Sherpa Van Trophy games.

**MOUNTFIELD, DEREK** After playing in only 30 games for Fourth Division Tranmere Rovers, Derek Mountfield joined Everton, the club he had supported as a schoolboy, for £30,000 in June 1982. Within five years at Goodison Park he had gained an FA Cup winners' medal, two League Championship medals, a European Cup Winners' Cup medal and two Charity Shield medals, not to mention two caps for England at 'B' and Under-21 level. During Everton's magnificent 1984–85 season he scored 14 goals from the centre-half position, including the last-minute equaliser against Ipswich in the FA Cup quarter-final and the semi-final extra-time winner against Luton Town. Following the arrival of Dave Watson he moved to Aston Villa where he established himself alongside Kent Nielsen, but after losing his place to Shaun Teale, he joined Wolverhampton Wanderers for £150,000 in November 1991. He made his début in a 3–2 home defeat by Derby County and over the next three seasons missed very few games as Wolves consolidated their position in the 'new' First Division. By the time Graham Taylor released him in the summer of 1994, Mountfield had made 91 appearances for the Molineux club. He joined Carlisle United and was a key member of their 1994–95 Championship-winning side. He later played for Northampton Town before signing for Walsall.

**MULLEN, JIMMY**  Jimmy Mullen is the youngest player ever to appear for Wolves in a first-class match. He was just 16 years and 43 days old when he played in the 4–1 win over Leeds United on 18 February 1939. During the Second World War he helped Wolves win the Wartime League (North) Cup in 1942 and, as well as 'guesting' for Leicester City, scored 27 goals in 87 games for the Molineux club. When league football resumed in 1946–47, the fast-raiding left-winger gave the club 13 seasons' service. He won the first of 12 full caps for England when he played against Scotland in April 1947 and his last seven years later, when he scored against Switzerland in the World Cup. He also had the distinction of being England's first-ever substitute when he replaced the injured Stan Mortensen against Belgium in May 1950. He scored in a 4–1 win. With Mullen on the left flank and Johnny Hancocks on the right, Wolves possessed the best pair of wingers in the Football League at that time. With Wolves, Mullen won three League Championship medals in 1953–54, 1957–58 and 1958–59 as well as an FA Cup winners' medal in 1949. He played the last of his 486 league and cup games, in which he scored 112 goals, in March 1959 as Wolves beat Arsenal 6–1.

**MUNRO, FRANK**  Frank Munro began his career as an amateur centre-forward with Chelsea but, after being released, returned north of the border to join Dundee United. Capped by Scotland at youth level, he was, surprisingly, allowed to join Aberdeen for £10,000 but after scoring a hat-trick against Wolves in a summer

*Frank Munro*

tournament in America in 1967, he joined the Molineux club for £55,000 in January 1968. He soon won over the Molineux faithful and over the next eight years gave the club great service. He appeared in the 1972 UEFA Cup final and the League Cup final victory over Manchester City two years later. Munro won nine full caps for Scotland during his stay at Molineux but, once he had helped them win the Second Division Championship in 1976–77, he left to join Celtic. Munro had scored 18 goals in 371 games for Wolves. He appeared for Celtic in the 1978 Scottish League Cup final before ending his playing days in Australian football.

**MURRAY, JIMMY** After making his Wolves début in a 2–0 home win over Charlton Athletic in November 1955, Jimmy Murray missed very few matches over the next eight seasons. In the opening game of the 1956–57 season, Murray scored four goals in a 5–1 defeat of Manchester City and ended the season with 17 goals in 33 games. When Wolves won the League Championship in 1957–58, Murray was the club's leading scorer with 32 goals in 45 games including hat-tricks against Birmingham City (Home 5–1) Nottingham Forest (Away 4–1) and Darlington in the FA Cup (Home 6–1). He was the club's leading scorer in the league the following season, when Wolves retained the Championship, with 21 goals in 28 games. In 1959–60, Murray again headed the goalscoring charts with 34 goals in 53 games and, though he finished behind Ted Farmer in 1960–61, his 23 goals in 31 league games included a hat-trick against Chelsea and a spell of eight goals in four games midway through the season. He headed the club's goalscoring list again in 1961–62 but in November 1963, after scoring 166 goals in 299 games, he was sold to Manchester City for £27,000. He made a sensational start to his Maine Road career, netting 12 goals in his first six matches including two hat-tricks, but after 43 goals in 70 games for City he was transferred to Walsall where he played out his league career. He then joined non-league Telford United and after helping the Shropshire club to successive FA Trophy finals at Wembley he hung up his boots.

**MUTCH, ANDY** Despite being an apprentice with both Everton and Liverpool, Andy Mutch was never offered professional terms and joined non-league Southport. His goalscoring talent was soon in evidence at Haig Avenue and, in February 1986, Wolves manager Sammy Chapman brought him to Molineux. He made his début the following month in a goalless home draw against Rotherham United but ended that disastrous relegation season with seven goals in 15 league games. Midway through the 1986–87 season he began to form a deadly scoring partnership with Steve Bull and though the

*Andy Mutch*

club were beaten by Aldershot in the play-offs, they won the Fourth Division Championship in 1987–88. That season the two strikers scored 53 of Wolves' 82 goals with Mutch's share being 19. The club also won the Sherpa Van Trophy in 1988 when Mutch scored the opening goal in the 2–0 win over Burnley in the Wembley final. Even more impressive in 1988–89, they netted 58 of the club's 96 goals to win the Third Division Championship. At the end of that season he earned recognition at England 'B' level when he appeared in three internationals. Continuing his high scoring record, he scored his first hat-trick for the club in a 6–2 home win over Newcastle United in March 1992. He had scored 105 goals in 338 first-team games for Wolves when, in the summer of 1993, he was surprisingly allowed to join Swindon Town for £250,000. He had scored 12 goals in 64 games when, just five games into the 1995–96 season, he was loaned to Wigan Athletic. After the clubs failed to agree terms, he returned to the County Ground before accepting a move to Stockport County. He soon burst into action with a hat-trick in a 4–2 win over promotion rivals Oxford United and later played an important role in the club winning promotion and reaching the semi-finals of the League Cup.

# N

**NEEDHAM, JACK** Jack Needham played his early football with Mansfield Town and Birmingham before joining Wolves in April 1910. He made a goalscoring début for the Molineux club in a 3–2 home win over Manchester City on the final day of the 1909–10 season. Throughout the following campaign he was the club's leading scorer with 13 goals, and in 1911–12 he scored his first hat-trick for the club in an 8–0 home win over Hull City. His best season for Wolves in terms of goals scored was 1914–15 when he netted 15 in 32 games including another hat-trick in a 7–2 defeat of Leicester Fosse. He was still a member of the Wolves side when league football resumed in 1919–20, but towards the end of that season he was transferred to Hull City where he ended his league career.

**NELSON, JACK** Chorley-born defender Jack Nelson began his career with his home-town club before joining Preston North End in March 1926. He appeared in 72 league games for the Lilywhites before moving to Wolverhampton Wanderers in November 1932. The Molineux club had just returned to top flight action and Nelson had been signed as cover for the club's centre-half spot, a position that was already being covered by Bellis, Pincott and Smith in the absence of the regular Hollingworth who was out of the side, injured. Nelson came into the side for the home match against Sunderland on 19 November 1932 – a game which the Wearsiders won 2–0 – and kept his place, helping the club in their fight against a quick return to the Second Division. Over the next couple of seasons he was an important member of the Wolves side but, after appearing in over 200 first-team games, he was allowed to leave Molineux and join Luton Town. In 1936–37 he helped the Hatters win the Third Division (South) Championship but after playing in 134 games he returned to Molineux as Wolves' trainer.

**NEUTRAL GROUNDS** Molineux has been used as a neutral ground for 11 FA Cup semi-finals from 1892 to 1957 and, as early as March 1891, it staged the England v Ireland international, watched by a crowd of 15,231. It has been the venue for a total of four full international matches, the last being played on 5 December 1956 when England beat Denmark 5–2 in a World Cup qualifier in front of 54,083 spectators. The ground has also housed three Inter-League games, Under-23 and Under-21 internationals, a wartime international and an amateur international. Wolverhampton Wanderers themselves have also had to replay on neutral ground a number of times.

| Date | Opponents | Venue | FA Cup | Score |
|------|-----------|-------|--------|-------|
| 29.02.1904 | Derby County | Villa Park | Rd 2 2R | 0–1 |
| 15.03.1937 | Sunderland | Hillsborough | Rd 6 2R | 0–4 |
| 01.03.1965 | Aston Villa | The Hawthorns | Rd 5 2R | 3–1 |
| 24.11.1986 | Chorley | Burnden Park | Rd 1 2R | 0–3 |

Once, also, in the League Cup:

| 18.12.1979 | Grimsby Town | Baseball Grd | Rd 5 2R | 2–0 |

The club's semi-finals were, of course, played on neutral grounds:

| Date | Opponents | Venue | Score |
|------|-----------|-------|-------|
| 16.03.1889 | Blackburn Rovers | Crewe | 1–1 |
| 23.03.1889 | Blackburn Rovers | Crewe | 3–1 |
| 08.03.1890 | Blackburn Rovers | County Ground, Derby | 0–1 |
| 04.03.1893 | Blackburn Rovers | Town Ground, Nottingham | 2–1 |
| 21.03.1896 | Derby County | Perry Barr | 2–1 |
| 28.03.1908 | Southampton | Stamford Bridge | 2–0 |
| 19.03.1921 | Cardiff City | Anfield | 0–0 |
| 23.03.1921 | Cardiff City | Old Trafford | 3–1 |
| 25.03.1939 | Grimsby Town | Old Trafford | 5–0 |
| 26.03.1949 | Manchester United | Hillsborough | 1–1 |
| 02.04.1949 | Manchester United | Goodison Park | 1–0 |
| 10.03.1951 | Newcastle United | Hillsborough | 0–0 |
| 14.03.1951 | Newcastle United | Leeds Road | 1–2 |
| 26.03.1960 | Aston Villa | The Hawthorns | 1–0 |
| 07.04.1973 | Leeds United | Maine Road | 0–1 |

| | | | |
|---|---|---|---|
| 31.03.1979 | Arsenal | Villa Park | 0–2 |
| 11.04.1981 | Tottenham Hotspur | Hillsborough | 2–2 |
| 15.04.1981 | Tottenham Hotspur | Highbury | 0–3 |
| 05.04.1998 | Arsenal | Villa Park | 0–1 |

The club's FA Cup final appearances at Kennington Oval, Fallowfield, Crystal Palace, Stamford Bridge and Wembley also qualify for inclusion, as do Wolves' appearances at the home of football in the League Cup final.

**NICKNAMES** Many players in the club's history have been fondly known by their nicknames. Some of the more unusual include:

| | | |
|---|---|---|
| Harry Wood | 1885–1898 | The Wolf |
| Ted Pheasant | 1896–1904 | Cock |
| Alf Tootill | 1928–1933 | The Birdcatcher |
| Billy Hartill | 1928–1935 | Artillery |
| Bert Williams | 1945–1957 | Cat |
| Les Wilson | 1965–1972 | The Reverend |
| Derek Parkin | 1967–1982 | Squeak |
| Keith Downing | 1987–1993 | Psycho |

**NON-LEAGUE** Non-League is the term used for clubs which are not members of the Football League. During the 1986–87 season, Wolves crashed out of the FA Cup to Chorley, losing a first-round tie 3–0 after a second replay in front of 5,421 spectators at Bolton's then Burnden Park home. The club's record against non-league opposition in the FA Cup since the Second World War is:

| Date | Opponents | Venue | Result |
|---|---|---|---|
| 22.01.1966 | Altrincham | Home | 5–0 |
| 15.11.1986 | Chorley | Burnden Park | 1–1 |
| 18.11.1986 | Chorley | Home | 1–1 |
| 24.11.1986 | Chorley | Burnden Park | 0–3 |
| 14.11.1987 | Cheltenham Town | Home | 5–1 |

# O

**OLDEST PLAYER** The oldest player to line-up in a Wolves first team is Lawrie Madden. He was 37 years 222 days old when he played his last game for the club against Derby County (Away 0–2) on 8 May 1993.

**OVERSEAS PLAYERS** Since South American Rafael Villazan played for Wolves in the early 1980s, there has been quite an influx of overseas players. Big Dutch defender John de Wolf, who won eight caps for Holland, joined Wolves from Feyenoord for £600,000 in December 1994. His time at Molineux was hampered by a number of injuries and after just 33 first-team appearances he left the club. Australian international Steve Corica joined the Wanderers from Leicester City for £1.1 million in February 1996. Formerly with Marconi of Sydney, he suffered cruciate knee ligament damage which has restricted his appearances to 57. Jens Dowe became the club's first German player when he arrived on loan from Hamburg in October 1996. After just eight appearances he went to Sturm Graz for £100,000. The deal was an expensive one for the Molineux club who paid £200,000 for his services to the end of the 1996–97 season! A free signing from French club Martigues, full-back Serge Romano made five appearances, three of which were as a substitute. He left Molineux in the summer of 1997 when his contract expired. Experienced Dutch keeper Hans Segers, who made his name with Wimbledon, replaced Mike Stowell for 13 matches during the 1997–98 season. Polish international full-back Darius Kubicki joined the club from Sunderland but after only 16 appearances was released and joined Tranmere Rovers. Spanish winger Izzy Diaz joined the club for a trial period but returned to Wigan Athletic after just one match, whilst Jesús Sanjuan was loaned from Real Zaragoza for three months but failed to make much impact. Finnish international centre-forward Mixu Paatelainen joined Wolves from Bolton Wanderers for £250,000 in the summer of 1997 and though he failed to score in the league, he netted four goals in the club's run to the FA Cup semi-finals. Full-back Kevin Muscat, the Australian international, joined the club from Crystal Palace in October 1997 in a £200,000 deal which also involved Dougie Freedman. Just after the start of the 1998–99 season, experienced Spaniard Fernando Gómez, who has represented his country at three different levels, joined the club and impressed during his first spell in English football. The club's latest acquisition is German Robert Niestroj, a £350,000 capture from Fortuina Dusseldorf.

**OWN GOALS** One of the fastest own goals in the Football League occurred on 4 February 1933 when Alf Young, the Huddersfield Town full-back, scored past his own keeper after just a few seconds of the match at Molineux. Before the first minute of the game had been played, the Yorkshire club equalised but Wolves went on to win 6–4. On 3 November 1971, Wolves beat Dutch side Den Haag 4–0 in the UEFA Cup second-round second-leg tie at Molineux to win 7–1 on aggregate. Den Haag had nevertheless given them a helping hand with three of Wolves' four second-leg goals being scored by Mansveldt, Weiner and Van Den Burgh!

# P

**PALMER, GEOFF** Only six players have made more appearances for Wolves than Geoff Palmer and it was with Derek Parkin, the man who has played more than any other, that Palmer formed an effective full-back partnership at Molineux. Palmer made his début for Wolves in a 2–1 defeat at Birmingham City in October 1973 and immediately made the right-back position his own. He played his part in the League Cup triumph against Manchester City at

*Geoff Palmer*

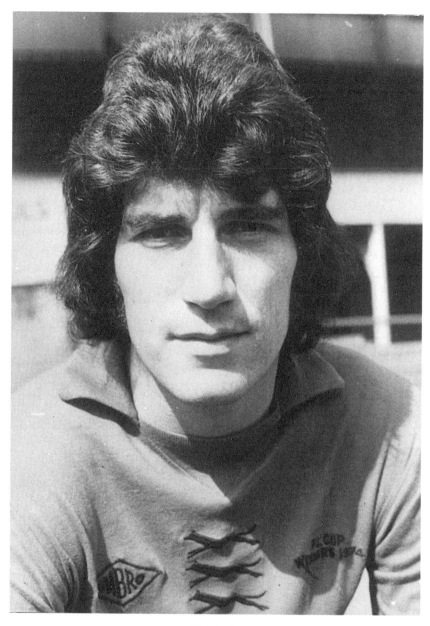

*Phil Parkes*

Wembley at the end of his first season. Palmer also impressed the International selectors and was capped twice for England at Under-23 level. After Wolves were relegated in 1976, they bounced straight back as Second Division champions in 1977, with Palmer playing every game alongside Parkin in League and Cup. He won a second League Cup winners' medal in 1980 as Wolves beat Nottingham Forest. After another relegation in 1982, Wolves came straight back up again, this time as runners-up, but were unable to sustain the recovery and were immediately relegated. After losing his first-team place to John Pender and with another relegation looming, Palmer left Molineux to join Burnley for £5,000. Unable to prevent the Clarets' relegation to the Fourth Division, he took the opportunity to return to Molineux as Wolves' player-coach in December 1985. Though he was able to win his place back in the Wolves defence, the club once again suffered relegation in 1986. Palmer, who had played in 496 first-team games, decided to retire and subsequently became a police officer in the West Midlands force.

**PARKES, PHIL** One of the club's tallest goalkeepers, Phil Parkes joined Wolves straight from school in 1962 and though he turned professional two years later, it was November 1966 before he made his début against Preston North End. To mark the occasion, he saved a penalty in a 3–2 win for Wolves. He went on to appear in 14 games that season as Wolves won promotion to the First Division. He missed very few games over the next nine seasons and was ever-present in 1971–72 and 1972–73, when he established a club record of 127 consecutive league appearances, breaking Noel George's record. Parkes won a UEFA Cup runners-up medal in 1972 but did not play at all in 1976–77 when the Molineux club won the Second Division title. He went on to appear in 382 first-team games. (Only Bert Williams has appeared in more matches for Wolves as a goalkeeper.) Having appeared for Vancouver Whitecaps, he returned there after his Molineux days were over and in 1979 helped them win the Soccer Bowl. He later played for Chicago Sting, San Jose Earthquakes and Toronto Blizzard.

**PARKIN, DEREK** The holder of the club appearance record, Derek Parkin played in 609 games for Wolves between 1968 and 1982. Signed from Huddersfield Town, Parkin made his début for the Molineux club in a 2–0 defeat at Newcastle United in February

141

*Derek Parkin*

1968. He was ever-present in seasons 1968–69 and 1969–70 and appeared in 116 consecutive league games from his début. He won League Cup winners' medals in 1974 and 1980 and won a Second Division Championship medal in 1976–77. Parkin's consistency led to his winning five England Under-23 caps as well as playing for the Football League but, sadly, full England honours never came his way. In 1972–73 Parkin was forced to miss over half the season by a mystery illness which at the time was diagnosed as a heart attack. Thankfully he regained full fitness and played in the Wolves side for a further nine seasons. In March 1982, he joined Stoke City for a fee of £40,000 and took his tally of league appearances for his three clubs to 602 before retiring at the end of the 1982–83 season.

**PEDLEY, JACK** Signed from Wednesbury Old Athletic as a replacement for Jack Miller, Jack Pedley made his first-team début in a 4–0 defeat at Liverpool in December 1905. He ended the season with 10 goals in 21 league outings including a hat-trick in a 6–1 win over Notts County. An ever-present in 1906–07, Pedley missed very few games over the next five seasons and in 1908 helped Wolves win the FA Cup as they beat Newcastle United 3–1 at Crystal Palace. Sadly, the pacy winger, who had scored 28 goals in 168 league and cup games, was forced to quit the game through injury in 1911 at the age of only 30.

**PEERS, TEDDY** Welsh international goalkeeper Teddy Peers began his career with Oswestry St Clairs before later playing for Chirk. After a trial with Shrewsbury Town, he played for three local clubs in his home town of Connah's Quay before joining Wolves in April 1911. He made his début on 2 March 1912, when he made a number of memorable saves in a 1–1 draw at home to Glossop. After that he was the club's first-choice keeper until the end of the 1920–21 season. Whilst with Wolves, Peers won eight full caps for Wales, his first against Ireland in 1913, and also played in two Victory Internationals in 1919. He had appeared in 198 League and Cup matches for Wolves when, in the summer of 1921, he left Molineux to join Port Vale. Though he added four more international caps to his collection, there could have been many more if only Vale had released him more often! After leaving Vale in 1923 he ended his professional career with Hednesford Town.

**PENALTIES**  Billy Heath of Wolverhampton Wanderers scored the first penalty in any Football League match in a 5–0 win against Accrington on 14 September 1891. When Wolves won the Second Division Championship in 1931–32, captain Wilf Lowton missed four spot-kicks, although he did score from nine attempts in the club's total of 115 goals. On Christmas Day 1936, in the Wolves v Huddersfield Town match at Molineux, Stan Cullis conceded an 86th minute penalty for handball. Bill Hayes scored past Alex Scott but Wolves won 3–1. On 2 October 1937 the same incident occurred again in the corresponding game at Leeds Road in the same minute involving the same three players. This time Huddersfield won 1–0. Full-back Cecil Shaw, who never missed a penalty when playing for Wolves, fluffed the first one he took after joining West Bromwich Albion in an FA Cup tie against Coventry City. On 27 September 1958 Wolves travelled to White Hart Lane where they lost 2–1 to Spurs. The Molineux club were awarded a penalty when Peter Broadbent was upended in the area by Spurs full-back Mel Hopkins. Bill Slater beat John Hollowbread with the penalty kick, only for the referee to disallow the 'goal' because three Wolves players had edged forward into the area. Slater took the second kick and saw Hollowbread save his high drive, much to the delight of the home crowd. This time a Spurs players had encroached into the box and the referee demanded that the kick be taken again. The Wolves captain Billy Wright asked Eddie Clamp to take the third kick and he beat the Spurs keeper with a shot that hit the upright before entering the net!

**PHEASANT, TED**  Ted 'Cock' Pheasant was a centre-half who captained Wolves a number of times during his eight seasons with the club. He joined Wolves from Wednesbury Old Athletic and made his début in the forward line in a 4–3 defeat at Derby County in September 1896. Injury prevented him from playing at all the following season but in 1898–99 he was the club's first-choice centre-half. Ted Pheasant was certainly a fearsome character and would shave his head and roll his sleeves up and his stockings down in order to strike terror into the hearts of the opposition forwards. He was also a dead-ball specialist and would take all the club's penalties and free-kicks. On 10 March 1902 he scored a hat-trick in Wolves' 3–0 win over Newcastle United, in which one of his goals came from a 30-yard free-kick. To commemorate this feat, he was awarded a specially inscribed gold watch by the Wolves chairman. Pheasant, who once turned down the chance to play for the Football League in order to turn out for his beloved Wolves, scored 19 goals in 168 League and Cup games before moving to West Bromwich Albion and later signing for Leicester Fosse. He never actually played for Leicester, for a couple of weeks after leaving The Hawthorns he died from peritonitis at the age of 33.

**PHILLIPS, CHARLIE** After winning schoolboy honours for Wales, Charlie Phillips worked as a boilerman and played Welsh League football for Ebbw Vale. His performances attracted a number of league clubs and though he had trials with Cardiff City, Plymouth Argyle and Torquay United, it was Wolves who secured his signature in August 1929. He made his début for the Molineux club in a 1–1 home draw against Oldham Athletic in March 1930 and soon became a great favourite with the fans. The ball-playing right-winger scored 18 goals in 37 games in 1931–32 as Wolves won the Second Division Championship, a campaign which also saw him score on his international début at Wrexham. Phillips, who was capped ten times during his Molineux career, had a very fiery temper and when Wolves played Bolton Wanderers on Boxing Day 1935, he was sent off whilst captaining the side. Within a few weeks, after having scored 65 goals in 202 games, he was on his way to Aston Villa for £9,000. Despite scoring on his début he couldn't prevent the Villans being relegated, although he did help them return to the top flight as Second Division Champions in 1937–38. At the end of that season he joined Birmingham but his stay at St Andrews was short and, after a spell with Chelmsford City, he 'guested' for a number of clubs during the Second World War.

**PHILLIPSON, TOM** One of the best strikers ever to play for Wolves, Tom Phillipson began his league career with Newcastle United before joining Swindon Town in the summer of 1921. In just over two seasons at the County Ground, he scored 26 goals in 87 games, this form prompting Wolves to pay £1,000 for his services in December 1923. He made his début in a 2–1 home win over Durham City on Christmas Day and ended the season in which Wolves won the Third Division (North) Championship with 14 goals in 28 games including a hat-trick in his fourth match when Ashington were beaten 7–1. Phillipson was the club's top scorer for the next three seasons and in 1925–26 netted 37 goals – a record which stood for 13 years until beaten by Dennis Westcott. During that season, in which Wolves finished fourth in Division Two, he scored four goals in a 7–1 defeat of Barnsley and hat-tricks against Middlesbrough (Home 3–1) and Stockport County (Home 5–1). He also found the net in 10 consecutive league games. In 1926–27, Phillipson scored 33 goals including five against Bradford City on Christmas Day when Wolves won 7–2, and hat-tricks against Barnsley (Home 9–1) and Clapton Orient (Home 5–0). Also that season he established a club record when he scored in 13 consecutive league games between 5 November 1926 and 9 February 1927. At the start of the 1927–28 season Phillipson was appointed captain of Wolves but midway through the campaign, after scoring 111 goals in 159 games, he left to join Sheffield United. He scored 25 goals in 56 league games for the Yorkshire club before moving to Walsall, where he ended his league career.

**PIERCE, GARY** Bury-born goalkeeper Gary Pierce played non-league football for Mossley before Huddersfield Town signed him as a full-time professional in 1969. After playing in 23 games for the Terriers he joined Wolves in the summer of 1973, primarily as cover for Phil Parkes. However, in September 1973 he replaced Parkes for six games, making his début in a 2–0 defeat at Newcastle United. Though he only appeared in 14 league games in that 1973–74 season, he played in the League Cup final at Wembley as Wolves beat Manchester City 2–1. He shared the goalkeeping duties with Phil Parkes for the next two seasons but in 1976–77 he was ever-present as Wolves won promotion to the top flight. Surprisingly, Wolves signed Paul Bradshaw and in 1977–78 Pierce failed to make a single appearance. In July 1979, after he had appeared in 111 first-team games, he left to join Barnsley, later ending his league career with Blackpool. Pierce then went into management with Accrington Stanley and later Radcliffe Borough.

**PITCH** The Molineux pitch measures 110 yards x 75 yards.

**PLASTIC** Four league clubs replaced their normal grass playing pitches with artificial surfaces at one stage or another. Queen's Park Rangers were the first in 1981 but the Loftus Road plastic was discarded in 1988 in favour of a return to turf. Luton Town (1985),

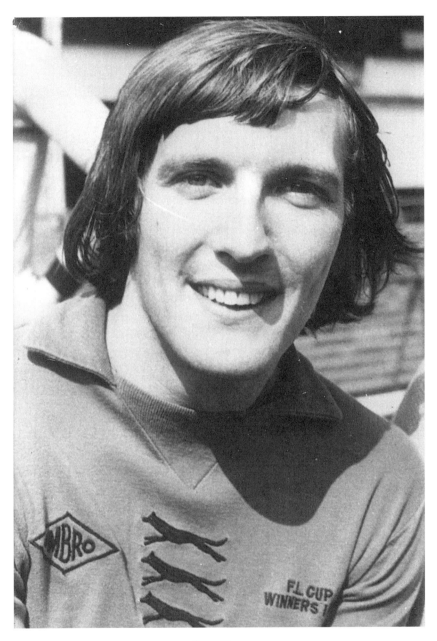

*Gary Pierce*

Oldham Athletic (1986) and Preston North End (1986) followed. Wolves never played on the Kenilworth Road plastic but their results on the other three grounds were as follows:

|  | P | W | D | L | F | A |
|---|---|---|---|---|---|---|
| Queen's Park Rangers | 2 | 0 | 0 | 2 | 2 | 4 |
| Oldham Athletic | 2 | 0 | 1 | 1 | 2 | 5 |
| Preston North End | 2 | 0 | 2 | 0 | 5 | 5 |

Though Wolves' record on plastic is not a good one, it is probably no worse than that of most clubs.

**PLAY-OFFS** Wolves were first involved in the play-offs at the end of the 1986–87 season when they finished fourth in Division Four. After beating Colchester United in the semi-final 2–0 on aggregate, the Molineux club surprisingly lost 3–0 on aggregate to Aldershot, who had finished nine points behind them. In 1994–95, Wolves finished fourth in Division One but went out at the semi-final stage of the play-offs losing 3–2 on aggregate to Bolton Wanderers after extra time, despite winning the first leg at Molineux 2–1. The club's last appearance in the play-offs was 1996–97 when, after finishing third in the First Division, they met Crystal Palace. After a 3–1 defeat at Selhurst Park in the first leg, Wolves were really up against it and, though they won the return match at Molineux 2–1, they went out 4–3 on aggregate.

**POINTS** Under the three-points-for-a-win system which was introduced in 1981–82, Wolves' best points tally was 92 points in 1988–89 when the club won the Third Division Championship. However, the club's best points haul under the former two-points-for-a-win system was 64 points in 1957–58 when they won the First Division championship. Wolves' worst record under either system was the meagre 23 points secured in 1905–06 when they finished 20th in the First Division and were relegated.

**PONTINS LEAGUE** Formerly the Central League, the competition was renamed the Pontins League for the start of the 1989–90 season when Wolves, who had left the Central League, returned to finish fourth in the Second Division and win promotion. However, in 1990–91 Wolves finished next to bottom in the First Division and returned to the Second Division. The following season they finished runners-up to Stoke City, albeit 12 points adrift of the Potters, to return to the First Division of the Pontins League. Since then, Wolves have continued to play in the First Division even after a Premier League was introduced, with their best position being fourth in 1993–94.

**POSTPONEMENT**  The bleak winter of 1962–63, described at the time as the 'Modern Ice Age', proved to be one of the most chaotic seasons in British soccer. The worst Saturday for league action in that awful winter was 9 February 1963 when only seven Football League fixtures went ahead. The worst Saturday for the FA Cup was 5 January 1963, the day of the third round, when only 3 of the 32 ties could be played. Wolves' match at Nottingham Forest had to be postponed five times and was eventually played on 29 January 1963 with Forest winning 4–3.

**POWELL, BARRY**  The son of Welsh international wing-half Ivor Powell, midfielder Barry Powell joined Wolves as an apprentice before signing professional forms in January 1972. He made his début as a substitute in a 1–1 draw at Crystal Palace in March 1973. He established himself as a first-team regular during the 1973–74 season and picked up a League Cup winners' medal as Wolves beat Manchester City 2–1. A few days later he won the first of four England Under-23 caps when Scotland were beaten 2–0. After he had spent the summer of 1975 playing in the NASL with Portland Timbers, he joined Coventry City for £75,000. In four years at Highfield Road he was a virtual ever-present, appearing in 164 league games, but in October 1979 he was transferred to Derby County for £340,000. Sadly the move did not work out, for at the end of his first season at the Baseball Ground the Rams were relegated and, in the summer of 1982, he signed for Bulova of Hong Kong. Two years later he returned to England and joined Burnley but seven months after that he had a spell at Swansea before rejoining his first club, Wolves. After ending his playing career at Molineux, where he took his total number of appearances for Wolves to 96, he was appointed to the club's coaching staff. Under manager Graham Turner he was part of the club's backroom team that masterminded Wolves to the championship of the Fourth Division and Sherpa Van Trophy success in 1988, as well as to the

Third Division Championship of 1989. He is now Football in the Community Officer at Coventry City.

**PRICE, FRED** England junior international Fred Price was a cultured right-half who joined Wolves from Dudley in June 1912. After making his first-team début in a 2–1 defeat at Grimsby Town in February 1913, he quickly established himself on the side and missed very few games before the outbreak of the First World War, being an ever-present in 1913–14. During the war years he served in the army and 'guested' for Port Vale but was still a regular on the Wolves side during the first season back after the hostilities. After 28 games, Price, who was struggling with a knee injury, lost his place to Val Gregory and in May 1920, after playing in 126 League and Cup games for Wolves, he left to join Port Vale. After just one season at Vale Park he moved to Newport County where he was forced to retire through injury and illness.

**PRITCHARD, ROY** A former Bevin Boy, full-back Roy Pritchard joined Wolves in 1941 and made 23 wartime appearances before making his league début in October 1946 as Wolves beat Huddersfield Town 6–1. It was midway through the 1947–48 season when Pritchard established himself as a first-team regular and over the next eight seasons he missed very few games. He won an FA Cup winners' medal in 1949 as Wolves beat Leicester City 3–1 in the Wembley final. When Wolves won their first League Championship in 1953–54, Pritchard appeared in 27 games. He had played in 223 League and Cup games for Wolves when in February 1956 he joined Aston Villa. Unfortunately he broke his jaw in his first game for Villa, against Arsenal, and after making just one appearance in each of three seasons, left to play for Notts County. He later played for Port Vale before joining non-league Wellington Town.

**PROMOTION** Wolves have been promoted on seven occasions. The first occasion was in 1923–24 when the club won the Third Division (North) Championship after just one season in that section. The club were promoted from the Second Division in 1931–32 as champions and repeated that move in 1966–67, 1976–77 and 1982–83 (but only in 1976–77 as champions). The club then won consecutive promotions in 1987–88 and 1988–89 as they moved from the Fourth to the Second Division.

**PURDIE, JON** An England Schoolboy international, Jon Purdie joined Arsenal as an apprentice in the summer of 1983 before turning professional in January 1985. However, his early promise was not fulfilled and he was given a free transfer when joining Wolves in July 1985. His first game for the Molineux club came in a 2–1 defeat at Brentford on the opening day of the 1985–86 season. That campaign saw Purdie play in 41 league games but at the end of the season Wolves were relegated to the Fourth Division for the first time in their history. In 1986–87 Purdie helped the club reach the play-offs but spent much of the following season – in which Wolves won the championship – either on the bench or on loan at Cambridge United. After scoring 13 goals in 103 games he moved to Oxford United in the summer of 1988 before later playing for Brentford and Shrewsbury. He then entered non-league football with Worcester City before joining Cheltenham town and Kidderminster Harriers, for whom he scored a spectacular winner in the club's FA Cup win over Birmingham City in January 1994.

**PYE, JESSE** Jesse Pye was an amateur with Sheffield United when the Second World War broke out and, after serving with the Royal Engineers in a number of countries, where he also got experience in Forces' football, he signed professional forms for Notts County. Whilst with the Meadow Lane club, Pye played for England against Belgium in a Victory International and in May 1946 Wolves beat off a number of leading clubs to secure his services for a fee of £12,000. He scored a hat-trick on his début as Wolves beat Arsenal 6–1 on the opening day of the 1946–47 season and ended the campaign with 21 goals including another treble in a 7–2 home win over Derby County. After scoring 16 league goals the following season, he was joint top scorer in 1948–49 with 21 goals when, after netting a hat-trick in a 7–1 win over Huddersfield Town, he scored two goals in the FA Cup final when Leicester City were beaten 3–1. In September 1949 he won his only full cap for England against the Republic of Ireland and ended the season as the club's top scorer with 18 goals, among which was another hat-trick against Huddersfield Town in a match that also ended in a 7–1 win for Wolves! Pye went on to score 95 goals in 209 League and Cup games before signing for Luton Town in the summer of 1952. He scored 31 goals in 60 games for the Hatters before moving to Derby County from where, after netting 24 goals in 61 games, he moved to Wisbech Town as player-manager.

# Q

**QUICKEST GOAL** Whilst there have undoubtedly been quicker goals scored by Wolves players, none have had such an adverse effect on the club as the one scored by Peter Knowles after just 35 seconds of the club's First Division match at Southampton on 18 September 1965, as the Saints went on to win 9–3.

# R

**RADFORD, WALTER** Wolverhampton-born forward Walter Radford had two spells with his home town club – the first was when he joined the Molineux staff in the summer of 1905. His first game in the Midland club's colours was in a 2–1 defeat at Woolwich Arsenal in February 1906 but, after playing in another game later in that campaign, he left Wolves to join Southampton. He failed to settle at The Dell and after scoring two goals in nine Southern League games he left the south coast club to return to Molineux for a second spell. In 1907–08 he scored 13 goals in 31 league and cup games and won an FA Cup winners' medal as Wolves beat Newcastle United 3–1 in the final at the Crystal Palace. The following season he was the club's leading scorer with 24 goals in 39 league and cup games including a hat-trick in a 5–3 win over Burnley at Turf Moor. He went on to score 48 goals in 94 games in his two spells with the club before joining Southport Central in June 1910. After retiring from the playing side of the game, he took up refereeing and later officiated in the Football League.

**RANKINE, MARK** Doncaster-born midfielder Mark Rankine began his Football League career with his home-town team Doncaster Rovers after having joined them as an apprentice in the summer of 1988. He appeared in 195 first-team games for the Belle Vue club before Wolves paid £70,000 for his services in January 1992. He made his début as a substitute in a 1–0 home win over Leicester City but then found himself in and out of the side over the next couple of seasons before establishing himself in the Wolves midfield in 1994–95. A hard-working player, he found himself switched to right-back the following season and this didn't help his performances. Rankine went on to appear in 167 games for the Molineux club before Preston North End paid £100,000 to take him to Deepdale. After a promising start, a hamstring injury led to his missing a number of games but now, after being transfer-listed during the summer of 1997, he is back to his best.

**RAPID SCORING** When Wolves entertained Manchester City on 18 August 1962 in the opening game of the 1962–63 season, they beat the Maine Road club 8–1 with Ted Farmer scoring four of the goals. Five of the club's goals came in a 14-minute spell either side of half-time. For the record, Wolves' other scorers that day were Murray (2), Hinton and Wharton.

**RECEIPTS** The club's record receipts are £276,168 which were for the FA Cup fourth round match against Tottenham Hotspur at Molineux on 7 February 1996.

**RELEGATION** Wolves have suffered the experience of relegation on eight occasions. The first was in 1905–06 when, after 18 seasons of First Division football, Wolves finished bottom of the league with just 23 points. Despite suffering some heavy defeats, Wolves won their last two home games against Notts County 6–0 and Derby County 7–1 but still went down. After 13 seasons of Second Division football, Wolves finished bottom in 1922–23 and were relegated to the Third Division (North) for the first time in their history. The club's next relegation came in 1964–65 when, after experiencing their longest spell in the top flight, they were relegated to the Second Division. After winning back their place in the First Division in 1966–67, the club had nine seasons in that section before suffering their fourth relegation in 1975–76. Winning promotion at the first attempt, Wolves then had five seasons of First Division football before another relegation in 1981–82. Again the club won immediate promotion but the club's worst-ever sequence of relegation was about to follow as they went from First Division to Fourth Division in consecutive seasons.

**RHODES, DICKY** A highly skilful half-back, Dicky Rhodes joined Wolves from Redditch United in the summer of 1926. In those days he played at centre-forward although, when he made his début in a 2–0 win at Chelsea in March 1929 he turned out at inside-right. Major Frank Buckley converted him into a half-back and, after establishing himself as a regular first-teamer in 1930–31, he helped

THE MOLINEUX ENCYCLOPEDIA

Wolves win the Second Division Championship the following season. During that campaign he missed just two games and went on to appear in 159 matches for the club before leaving to join Sheffield United in October 1935. He later played for Swansea Town before hanging up his boots shortly before the outbreak of the Second World War. Dicky Rhodes became a champion canary breeder, winning the national title in 1973 when he beat off the challenge of 1,500 competitors at London's Alexandra Palace.

**RICHARDS, DAI**  Welsh international Dai Richards joined Wolves from Third Division (South) side Merthyr Town in the summer of 1927 and made his début as inside-right in February 1928 in a 2–2 draw at Port Vale. It was his only appearance in the Wolves side that season but once Major Frank Buckley had converted him into a wing-half he began to play on a more regular basis. Forming a good understanding with Charlie Phillips, Richards missed very few games for Wolves over the next eight seasons and was a key member of the club's Second Division Championship-winning side of 1931–32. Richards went on to score five goals in 229 league and cup games for Wolves before being transferred to Brentford in November 1935 for a fee of £3,500. Unable to settle in London, he joined Birmingham on the morning of their match against Brentford and in the afternoon played against his former colleagues in a 4–0 win for the St Andrews side. He later played for Walsall but his career was interrupted by the Second World War and, by the time league football resumed in 1946–47, he was too old.

**RICHARDS, DICK**  Another Welsh international, Dick Richards began his footballing career with Bronygarth FC before playing for Chirk and Oswestry United, from where he signed for Wolverhampton Wanderers in the summer of 1913. Though he only appeared in 13 games prior to the outbreak of the First World War, he was the club's leading scorer in 1919–20 with 10 goals. The following season he scored one of the goals in Wolves' 3–1 FA Cup semi-final replay win over Cardiff City but missed the final against Tottenham Hotspur. Richards, who won five caps whilst with Wolves, played his early international football alongside other Molineux favourites in Teddy Peers and Ted Vizard. He had scored 26 goals in 94 games when in June 1922 he left Wolves to join West Ham United. He played for the Hammers in the 'White Horse' FA

*John Richards*

Cup final of 1923 but after 53 games for the Upton Park club he left to join Fulham. He later played for Mold Town and Colwyn Bay before a back injury forced his retirement. The last of Richards' nine Welsh caps came in 1926 when he was playing for Mold, the only time a player from that club has achieved full international honours.

**RICHARDS, JOHN** One of the most prolific scorers in the history of Wolverhampton Wanderers, John Richards joined the Molineux club on leaving school in Warrington in 1967 and turned professional two years later. He made his début in the gold and black colours at The Hawthorns in February 1970, a match Wolves drew 3–3. Forming a great partnership with Derek Dougan, it was 1971–72 before he established himself as a regular first-teamer, scoring 16 goals in 48 games and gaining a UEFA Cup runners-up medal. The following season he was the country's leading scorer with 33 league and cup goals and another three in the Texaco Cup. His total included hat-tricks against Stoke City (Home 5–3) and Everton (Home 4–2). At the end of that season he won his only England cap when he played in a 2–1 win over Northern Ireland. In 1974 he scored the winning goal in Wolves' 2–1 win over Manchester City in the League Cup final and in 1976–77 he helped the club win the Second Division Championship. In 1980 he was a member of the Wolves side that beat Nottingham Forest 1–0 in the League Cup final. The only player to have received two benefits at Wolves – in 1982 and 1986, the second coming some three years after he had left the club, he went on to score 194 goals in 486 games before leaving Molineux in unhappy circumstances. He joined Portuguese side Maritimo in the summer of 1983 after a loan spell at Derby County and spent three years there before returning to work for Wolverhampton Leisure Services Department. He is now the Molineux club's managing director.

**RILEY, ALF** Though he stood only 5ft 7ins, Alf Riley was Wolves' centre-half before and after the First World War. The Stafford-born defender had begun his playing career with Stafford Excelsior and Stafford Rangers but was on Wellington Town's books when Wolves signed him in July 1913. He made his league début for the Molineux club in a 2–2 home draw against Huddersfield Town in April 1914 and appeared in 11 first-team games before the First World War. When league football resumed after the hostilities, Riley became the club's regular left-half and went on to appear in 130 games. His only goal came on 30 April 1921 in a 3–0 home win over Leicester City. Riley, who won an FA Cup runners-up medal in 1921, was forced to retire through injury at the end of the 1922–23 season, having played his last game at Notts County in November 1922.

**ROBERTSON, ALLY** A Scottish Schoolboy international, Ally Robertson joined West Bromwich Albion as an apprentice in the

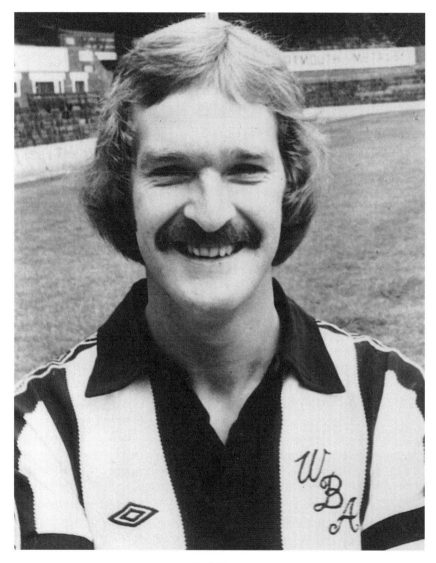

*Ally Robertson*

summer of 1968 and a year later signed professional forms. He made his league début for the Baggies in October 1969, starring in a 2–1 win over Manchester United. He then won six Scottish Youth international caps but, just when the future seemed rosy, he broke his leg playing in a League Cup tie against Charlton Athletic. He soon bounced back, however, and by 1972 he had established himself as first-choice central defender alongside John Wile. This partnership was to last until 1983 when Wile left Albion to return to Peterborough United as player-manager. With West Brom, Robertson played in three losing major Cup semi-finals and broke the club record of consecutive league appearances held by Jimmy Dudley. He had appeared in 626 games for Albion when he was given a free transfer in the summer of 1986 and joined Wolves. His first game for the Molineux club was in a 1–0 home defeat by Burnley in September 1986, after which he played in a further 30 games as Wolves won a place in the promotion play-offs. In 1987–88 he appeared in 41 league games as the club won the Fourth Division Championship and 30 the following season as Wolves took the Third Division title by storm. He took his total number of games for Wolves to 134 before leaving to go into management with non-league Worcester City.

**ROSE, BILLY** Billy Rose was Wolves' first international goalkeeper. He won four caps for England before he joined Wolves, winning his first against Ireland in February 1884. He began his career with Small Heath before joining the Swifts club of London where his performances brought him to the attention of a number of top clubs. Before signing for Wolves he played for Wiltshire, Staffordshire and London and appeared for Preston North End and Stoke. He joined Wolves in January 1889 and played in four games during the club's first Football League campaign. Over the next five seasons, he was a virtual ever-present in the Molineux club's side. He won a fifth cap for England whilst with Wolves, playing against Ireland at Molineux, and won an FA Cup winners' medal in 1893 as Everton were beaten 1–0. He missed the entire 1894–95 season when he played for Loughborough Town following a disagreement with the Wolves committee over his proposal to form a Players' Union. He returned to Molineux in 1895 and played the last of his 155 League and Cup games against Small Heath, exactly seven years since joining the club, in a match Wolves won 7–2.

**RUNNERS-UP** Wolverhampton Wanderers have been runners-up in the First Division on five occasions and have twice won promotion to the top flight after finishing the season as runners-up in the Second Division.

# S

**SCOTCHBROOK, FRED** Fred Scotchbrook joined Bolton Wanderers just before the outbreak of the First World War but after only five appearances in the Wanderers side he decided he was not good enough for that standard of football and retired to concentrate on coaching. He remained at Burnden Park as coach and then assistant-secretary before joining Stockport County as manager in November 1924. In 1924–25 County finished in a disappointing 19th place, only three points above the relegation position. Scotchbrook's second season with the club was even worse, as they lost six of their first seven fixtures, but though he was sacked in February 1926 County still finished bottom of the Second Division. His record at Edgeley Park did not deter Wolverhampton Wanderers from appointing him manager, though he was never given full control at Molineux and became disheartened when directors would make decisions at a whim, which he could do nothing to prevent. Scotchbrook blamed the directors for the club's lack of success and left soon after criticising club policy at the annual meeting in the summer of 1927.

**SCOTT, ALEX** Originally a centre-half, goalkeeper Alex Scott won England Schoolboy honours and played soccer for Forest Dynamos before joining his home-town team, Liverpool, in 1930. However, competition at Anfield was stiff and after understudying Elisha Scott (no relation) he left to join Burnley in the summer of 1933. He appeared in 60 games for the Turf Moor club before signing for Wolves in February 1936 for a fee of £1,250. His first game for the Molineux club came in a goalless draw at home to Derby County, after which he appeared in 129 League and Cup games up to the outbreak of the Second World War. During this period he won an FA Cup runners-up medal after Portsmouth had beaten Wolves 4–1

*Second Division champions 1976–77*

in the 1939 final. Scott was a tall, powerfully built goalkeeper with the ability to kick the ball the full length of the field, often clearing the opposing keeper's crossbar! He was sent off whilst playing for Wolves at Huddersfield Town on 28 December 1936, a match which the club went on to lose 4–0. He continued to play for the club during the war years before leaving to join Crewe Alexandra in August 1947. Alex Scott was also a fine baseball pitcher and represented England in 12 internationals.

**SECOND DIVISION** Wolves have had seven spells in the Second Division. Their first, following relegation in 1905–06, lasted for 13 seasons until they were relegated to the Third Division (North) in 1922–23. After winning promotion at the first attempt, Wolves embarked on their second spell in Division Two in 1924–25, winning the Championship eight seasons later and so finally regaining their place in the First Division after an absence of 26 years. The club's third spell in Division Two lasted just two seasons, since after relegation in 1964–65 the club finished as runners-up to

Coventry City in 1966–67 and regained their place in the top flight. After nine seasons of First Division football, Wolves were relegated to the Second Division but their fourth spell lasted only a season as they won the championship in style. The club's fifth spell in the Second Division was also for one season as Wolves finished runners-up to Queen's Park Rangers in 1982–83. Relegated after just one season, Wolves' sixth spell in Division Two in 1984–85 also brought relegation as the club entered the Third Division for only the second time in their history. After a number of relegation- and promotion-winning seasons, Wolves found themselves in the Second Division for the 1989–90 campaign and have remained in that section, although under reorganisation it is now the 'new' First Division.

**SEMI-FINALS** Up to the end of the 1998–99 season, Wolverhampton Wanderers had been involved in 14 FA Cup semi-finals, three League Cup semi-finals, a European Cup Winners' Cup and a UEFA Cup semi-final. They have also reached that stage of the Texaco Cup and Sherpa Van Trophy competitions.

**SHAW, BERNARD** Sheffield-born full-back Bernard Shaw began his league career with his home-town club Sheffield United and had made 134 league appearances for the Blades when he signed for Wolves in the summer of 1969. However, he had to wait before making his league début for the Molineux club until October of that year, when Wolves drew 2–2 against the other club from the city of his birth, Sheffield Wednesday. The following season he helped the club win the Texaco Cup, whilst in 1971–72 he won a UEFA Cup runners-up medal as Wolves lost to Spurs over two legs. He went on to appear in 156 games before being transferred to Sheffield Wednesday in May 1973. He played in 113 games for the Owls before the Hillsborough club released him in the summer of 1976 when they had slumped towards the foot of the Third Division.

**SHAW, CECIL** Mansfield-born Cecil Shaw had played his early football with a number of local clubs as centre-forward but after signing for Wolves in February 1930 he was converted into a full-back. His first game for the club came in the final game of the 1930–31 season when Wolves lost 2–0 at Hull City. Over the next two seasons he was in and out of the side but made 10 appearances in 1931–32 when the club won the Second Division Championship.

After that he established himself as a first-team regular and missed very few games in the next four seasons. An ever-present in seasons 1934–35 and 1935–36, he appeared in 121 consecutive league games for Wolves, but in May 1936 – after playing in 183 games – he joined West Bromwich Albion. Having scored eight goals from the penalty spot and never missed, Shaw fluffed the first one he ever took for the Baggies! He made 127 appearances for Albion and after 'guesting' for Blackpool in the Second World War he played non-league football for Hereford United.

**SHAW, HAROLD** Wolves manager George Jobey signed left-back Harold Shaw from his home-town team of Hednesford United in the summer of 1923 and, after making his début for the Molineux club in a goalless draw at Chesterfield on the opening day of the 1923–24 season, he went on to appear in 37 games as the club won the Third Division (North) Championship. Forming good full-back partnerships, first with Ted Watson and then with Len Williams, Shaw was a virtual ever-present in the Wolves side for the next ten seasons and appeared in 249 League and Cup games before Major Frank Buckley sold him to Sunderland in February 1930 for a fee of £7,000. After making his début for the Wearsiders in the local derby against Newcastle United, which the Magpies won 3–0, he was an ever-present in 1931–32 and scored the first goal of his career in a 4–2 defeat at Everton – his career with Wolves had been goalless. He was with Sunderland when they won the League Championship in 1935–36 but on the sidelines when they won the FA Cup the following season. He retired shortly afterwards, having scored five goals in 217 first-team games.

**SHELTON, JACK** After making his début against Derby County in October 1907 at right-half, Jack Shelton was moved into the Wolves' forward line with great effect and, in only his fifth game as inside-forward, he scored a hat-trick in a 5–1 home win over Grimsby Town. He ended the season with nine goals in 24 league games and won an FA Cup winners' medal as Wolves beat Newcastle United in the final at the Crystal Palace 3–1. Throughout his time at Molineux, Shelton was more a maker than a scorer of goals and when he left to join Port Vale in August 1910 he had found the net 17 times in 94 first-team outings. With the Valiants he was on the sides which won the Staffordshire Cup and the Birmingham Cup, and after 'guesting' for Stoke during the 1915–16 season he returned to the club for the following campaign in which he was ever-present. He was conscripted in the summer of 1917, however, and was killed in action in September 1918.

**SHERPA VAN TROPHY** The competition for Associate Members of the Football League was first sponsored by Sherpa Van in the 1987–88 season. Wolves' first match in the Sherpa Van Trophy saw them draw 1–1 at Swansea City before beating Bristol City 3–1 at Molineux to qualify for the knockout stages. In the first-round match at home to Brentford, Steve Bull netted a hat-trick in a 4–0 win for Wolves. They repeated the scoreline in the Southern Section quarter-final against Peterborough United, in which Bull grabbed two of the goals. It was Steve Bull that separated the teams when Wolves met Torquay United in the Area semi-final to set up a two-legged Area final against Notts County. The first leg at Meadow Lane ended all square at 1–1, whilst the return at Molineux saw Wolves win 3–1 to go through to the Wembley final against Burnley. Steve Bull, who had scored in every round of the competition, found the net on 12 occasions. Nevertheless, despite the fact that he did not score in the final, Wolves outplayed their Lancashire opponents in front of an 80,841 crowd, and won 2-0 with goals from Mutch and Dennison. In 1988–89, the holders again qualifed for the knockout stages after drawing 2–2 at Hereford United and beating Port Vale at Molineux 5–1, a match in which Steve Bull scored four goals. Bull netted a hat-trick in a 3–0 first-round defeat of Bristol City and then created all three goals for Dennison, Gooding and Vaughan in a 3–1 extra-time win over Northampton Town. A 2–0 win over Hereford United took Wolves into the Southern Section final where they met Torquay United over two legs. After winning 2–1 at Plainmoor, with Steve Bull scoring both goals, it looked as if Wolves would be going to Wembley for a second successive season, but the Devon club won 2–0 in front of a Molineux crowd of 22,532 to win through to the final where they went down 4–1 to Bolton Wanderers.

**SHORT, JOHN** Barnsley-born defender John Short made his league début for Wolves on 2 December 1950, the day Johnny Hancocks's hat-trick helped beat West Bromwich Albion 3–1. He held his place and appeared in all of the club's seven FA Cup games as they reached the semi-finals where they lost 2–1 to Newcastle United after a replay. After spending much of the 1951–52 season deputising for Gus McLean or Roy Pritchard, he was asked to help the club out by playing as an emergency centre-forward in the FA Cup third-round replay against Manchester City. He responded by scoring two goals in a 4–1 win before reverting to his defensive role. When Wolves won their first ever League Championship in 1953–54, Short appeared in 26 games. He went on to play in 107 League and Cup games for the Molineux club before leaving to join Stoke City. He made 55 appearances for the Potters before moving to his hometown team, Barnsley, where he played in 109 games before hanging up his boots.

**SHORTHOUSE, BILL** Nicknamed 'The Baron', Bill Shorthouse joined Wolves as an amateur in June 1941. He served in the army and was wounded on the Normandy beaches on 'D' Day. Once he was demobbed, he signed professional forms for the Molineux club and after several games for Wath Wanderers, the club's nursery side, he made his league début in a 4–3 defeat at Manchester City on the opening day of the 1947–48 season. In that game he played at left-back but three months later he replaced Gordon Brice at centre-half and remained a regular first-team member for the next nine seasons of league football. In 1949 he won an FA Cup winners' medal as Wolves beat Leicester City 3–1. When Wolves won the League Championship for the first time in 1953–54, Shorthouse missed just two league games. The following season saw him revert to left-back when Billy Wright took over the number five shirt. He played the last of his 379 League and Cup games against Birmingham City at Molineux in September 1956, his only goal for the club coming in a 2–0 home win over Charlton Athletic in November 1955. When he hung up his boots, he did so with the distinction of never having been dropped by Wolves, only missing a handful of games through injury or illness. After leaving Molineux he became coach to the England Youth team and also served both Birmingham City and Aston Villa in that capacity – in fact, he was in charge when Villa won the FA Youth Cup in 1980.

**SHOWELL, GEORGE** George Showell began his Football League career with Wolverhampton Wanderers but spent most of his early days at Molineux playing in the club's Central League side. After making his first-team début in a 1–1 draw against Preston North

End in April 1955, he did his National Service – but he still had to wait until 1959–60 before claiming a regular place. In 1958–59 he was tried as an emergency striker and responded with two goals in four games against Arsenal (Away 1–1) and Birmingham City (Home 3–1). In his first full season on the Wolves side, he helped the Molineux club finish runners-up in the First Division and win the FA Cup, beating Blackburn Rovers in the final. He went on to play in 218 League and Cup games before deciding to leave Molineux in May 1965 and join Bristol City. His stay at Ashton Gate was short and he then moved to North Wales to play for Wrexham. Sadly, after just two seasons at the Racecourse Ground in which he played 54 games, he was forced to quit the playing side with a serious knee injury. He was then taken on to the coaching staff and later became trainer, caretaker-manager and physiotherapist in 24 years' service to the Robins. Unfortunately he had to resign his post in 1990, as he was considered unqualified under the new rules laid down by the FA.

**SIDLOW, CYRIL** Though Welsh international goalkeeper Cyril Sidlow only appeared in four league games for the Molineux club, he did appear in 94 games during the Second World War. Colwyn Bay-born Sidlow began his career with his home-town club before playing for a number of other Welsh clubs including Abergele, Flint Town and Llandudno Town. He joined Wolves in the summer of 1937 and made his début in a 3–2 home win over Birmingham in April 1938. Two games later he was between the posts as Wolves beat Leicester City 10–1. As well as appearing for Wolves during the war years, Sidlow 'guested' for Darlington, Notts County and Wrexham. With Wolves he won a Wartime League Cup winners' medal in 1942 and played in 11 Wartime and Victory internationals. In December 1946, Sidlow joined Liverpool for a goalkeeper's record fee of £5,000. He made 165 appearances for the Anfield club between 1946 and 1951, winning a League Championship medal and an FA Cup runners-up medal as well as seven Welsh caps. He could be inconsistent at times, but will always be remembered as one of the first goalkeepers to throw the ball out of his area rather than just kick it upfield.

**SLATER, BILL** Bill Slater joined Blackpool as a schoolboy soon after the war and made his league début for the Seasiders in September 1949 in a goalless draw at Aston Villa. As a nippy inside-forward, he found himself competing with Allan Brown for the number ten shirt but, unable to be guaranteed a first-team place, he joined Brentford in December 1951. Slater holds two interesting records – he is the last amateur to have appeared in an FA Cup final at Wembley, for Blackpool in 1951; and he scored Blackpool's quickest-ever goal which came after only 11 seconds of their game against Stoke City in December 1949. Unable to settle at Griffin Park, he joined Wolves in August 1952 and signed semi-professional forms in February 1954. He had made his first-team début in a 6–2 home win over Manchester United. When Wolves won the League Championship for the first time in 1953–54, Slater, who missed just three games, played at wing-half. Capped 21 times by England as an amateur, he won the first of 12 full caps in November 1954 when he played in a 3–1 win over Wales at Wembley. He won further League Championship medals in 1957–58 and 1958–59 and in 1960 was voted Footballer of the Year after actually starting the season in the club's Central League side. He had scored 25 goals in 339 games for Wolves when he left Molineux in the summer of 1963 to rejoin Brentford. After just one season he played for Northern Nomads before hanging up his boots in late 1964. He then became deputy director of the Crystal Palace sports centre and later worked as director of physical education at Liverpool and Birmingham Universities. In 1982 he was awarded the OBE for his services to sport and, after five years as director of National Services, he was elected president of the British Gymnastics Association.

**SMALLEY, TOM** Wing-half Tom Smalley joined Wolves from South Kirkby Colliery near Barnsley in May 1931 and made his début for the Molineux club in a 4–2 defeat at Preston North End on 5 February 1932. Strong in the tackle, Smalley established himself in the Wolves side during the 1933–34 season and missed very few games in the five seasons that followed. He was ever-present in 1935–36 when Wolves finished 15th in the First Division. During that campaign he was used as an emergency centre-forward and, in a seven-game spell, scored six goals. Early the following season he won his only full cap for England when he played against Wales at Molineux. He had scored 12 goals in 196 League and Cup games for Wolves when he was allowed to leave the club and join Norwich City in the summer of 1938. He played in 43 league games for the Canaries before joining Northampton Town during the early part of the Second World War. As well as playing for the Cobblers during the war years, he 'guested' for West Bromwich Albion but returned to the County Ground when league football resumed in 1946–47. He went on to appear in exactly 200 league games for Northampton before leaving to become player-coach at Lower Gornal.

**SMITH, JACK** One of the smallest players to represent the club, Jack Smith played his early football for Cannock and Stafford Road FC before joining Wolves in the summer of 1902. He made his début in the opening game of the 1902–03 season and scored two goals in a 3–0 home win over Derby County. Forming a good left-wing partnership with John Miller, he was joint top scorer for the club with Billy Wooldridge in 1904–05 when both forwards found the net 14 times. He had scored 43 goals in 114 League and Cup games for Wolves when, following their relegation to the Second Division in 1906, he left Molineux to sign for Birmingham. His stay at St Andrews was brief and in March 1907 he joined Bristol Rovers, for whom he netted 10 goals in 31 games before ending his career with Norwich City, where he scored 24 goals in 41 appearances for the Canaries.

**SMITH, LES** Halesowen-born winger Les Smith joined Wolves as an amateur in the summer of 1945 and turned professional in 1946. He had to wait until April 1948 before making his league début for Wolves when they won 3–2 at home to Stoke City. Over the next three seasons he appeared in only a handful of games but in 1951–52, when he was given an extended run in the side, he scored seven goals in a nine-game spell. When Wolves won the League Championship in 1953–54 Smith only played in four games but missed only eight two seasons later when the club were runners-up in the First Division. He had scored 24 goals in 94 games for the Molineux club when Aston Villa paid £25,000 for his services in February 1956. He won an FA Cup winners' medal in 1957 and went on to score 25 goals in 130 first-team outings for Villa before an Achilles tendon injury forced him to retire from the game in January 1960.

**SMYTH, SAMMY** A prolific goalscorer with Distillery, Sammy Smyth was playing as an amateur for Linfield when Wolves manager Ted Vizard wanted to sign him for Wolves. His transfer to the Molineux club was unusual in that Smyth had to turn professional with an Irish club before Wolves could sign him on similar forms. So he signed for Dunella and within an hour or so had joined Wolves for a fee of £1,100, surely the shortest time that a professional has ever spent with one club! He made his début in a 4–3 defeat at Manchester City on the opening day of the 1947–48 season before scoring twice in his first home appearance four days later as Grimsby Town were beaten 8–1. In 1948–49 he scored 22 goals in 46 league and cup games to top the club's scoring charts, including one of the finest individual goals ever seen at Wembley as Wolves beat Leicester City 3–1 to lift the FA Cup. Smyth, who spent five seasons at Molineux and scored 43 goals in 116 games, won nine full caps for Northern Ireland and eight whilst with Wolves. He eventually left Molineux in September 1951 to join Stoke City for £20,000. He scored 19 goals in 44 first-team outings for the Potters before another move took him to Liverpool. He had scored 20 goals in 45 league games for the Anfield club, but in May 1954 he returned to Ireland to play for Bangor City whom he joined for a then record fee for an Irish League club of £2,000.

**SONGS** When Wolves won the League Championship in 1953–54 they beat their arch rivals West Bromwich Albion home and away, and after beating a number of top foreign sides, a new song was heard at Molineux, sung to the tune of the 'Happy Wanderer':

> *Who's the team, the wonder team,*
> *The team in gold and black,*
> *They knocked four points off the Albion,*
> *And beat Honved and Spartak.*

**SPONSORS** The club's sponsors are Good Year. Previous sponsors include Manders Paint, Staw and Tatung, who were the club's first sponsors.

**STOBART, BARRY** Barry Stobart joined Wolves' nursery side Wath Wanderers in 1953 when he was 15 and turned professional two years later. He had to wait until March 1960 before making his league début, when he scored Wolves' second goal in a 2–0 win at Manchester United. He also scored on his home début when Wolves drew 3–3 with Preston North End. Stobart had only made five first-team appearances when manager Stan Cullis called him into the club's FA Cup final side against Blackburn Rovers in 1960 as a late replacement for the injured Bobby Mason. He helped Wolves win 3–0 to earn himself an FA Cup winners' medal. He went on to score 22 goals in 54 games before joining Manchester City in August 1964 for £20,000. His stay at Maine Road lasted just four months, for in December 1964 he signed for Aston Villa. He later played for Shrewsbury Town before managing non-league sides Willenhall Town and Dudley Town.

**STOUTT, STEVE** Halifax-born defender Steve Stoutt began his Football League career as a non-contract player with Huddersfield Town but, after only 10 appearances for the Yorkshire club, he joined Wolverhampton Wanderers towards the end of the 1984–85 season, a campaign which saw the club relegated to the Third Division. Though he played in 28 games the following season, he couldn't prevent the club from suffering a further relegation, this time to the Fourth Division for the first time in their history. In 1986–87 he played an important part in the club getting to the play-offs and had an outstanding first half of the 1987–88 season as Wolves won the Fourth Division Championship before injury ruled him out of the run-in. In August 1988, after appearing in 117 games for Wolves, he joined Grimsby Town but he found it difficult to hold down a first-team place with the Mariners and moved to Lincoln City where he ended his league career.

**STOWELL, MIKE** Goalkeeper Mike Stowell played non-league football for Leyland Motors before signing for Everton on professional forms in December 1985. Throughout his five years at Goodison Park he was an understudy to the brilliant Welsh international keeper Neville Southall and only made one first-team appearance, keeping a clean sheet against Millwall in the Simod Cup. He did however have loan spells with Chester City, York City, Manchester City, Port Vale, Wolves and Preston North End before Graham Turner signed him for the Molineux club on a permanent basis in July 1990. Stowell, who cost Wolves £275,000, had made seven appearances on loan towards the back end of the 1988–89 season but his form was such that in his first few matches after joining the club from Everton he was named in the England 'B' squad. A good shot-stopper, he was the club's only ever-present in

*Mike Stowell*

1996–97 and at the time of writing has appeared in 366 first-team games for the Molineux club.

**STREETE, FLOYD** Jamaican-born defender Floyd Streete played his early football with the Rivet Sports Club before signing professional forms with Cambridge United in the summer of 1976. He spent seven years at the Abbey Stadium and in his first season with the club he helped them win the Fourth Division Championship. The following season he helped the Us win promotion to Division Two. After 125 league appearances for Cambridge he went to play abroad with Utrecht and SC Cambuur before Derby County signed him on a non-contract basis in September 1984. He appeared in 35 league games for the Rams before Bill McGarry paid just £5,000 to bring him to Molineux in October 1985. He made his début in a 2–1 win at Rotherham United and, though the club were relegated at the end of that season, Streete turned in a number of outstanding performances, albeit with a variety of central defensive partners. After helping the club into the Fourth Division play-offs in 1986–87, he was a member of the Wolves side that won the Fourth Division Championship, the Sherpa Van Trophy in 1987–88 and the Third Division title the following season. Streete went on to play in 159 games for Wolves before leaving to join Reading in July 1990.

**STUART, EDDIE** South African-born Eddie Stuart joined Wolves from Rangers FC of Johannesburg, where the club's coach was the former Bolton Wanderers player Billy Butler. Stuart made his début for Wolves at centre-forward and scored their goal in a 4–1 home defeat by West Bromwich Albion on 15 April 1952. He did not appear at all the following season but in 1953–54 played at right-back in the last 12 games of the season, helping the club win the League Championship. After that, Stuart was a virtual ever-present in the number two shirt for the next 11 seasons and appeared in 322 League and Cup games. Though he won further League Championship medals in 1958 and 1959, and played in Europe, he did not play in the 1960 FA Cup final win over Blackburn Rovers, when George Showell was preferred. Stuart left Molineux in the summer of 1962 to become one of the final pieces in the jigsaw assembled by Tony Waddington at Stoke City. The dominating defender was immediately made captain and led the Potters to the Second Division Championship in his first season at the Victoria Ground. However, at the age of 33 and with the pace in the top flight telling, he moved to Tranmere Rovers for £4,000 and later to

Stockport County where he won a Fourth Division Championship medal in 1966–67. After retiring from the Football League he became player-manager at Worcester City.

**SUBSTITUTES** The first ever Wolverhampton Wanderers substitute was Fred Goodwin, who came on for Ernie Hunt against Middlesbrough at Molineux on 16 October 1965. The club had to wait until 2 September 1967 for their first goalscoring substitute – Les Wilson – who scored in a 4–2 defeat at Everton. The only Wolves substitute to score a hat-trick is John Richards in the fifth-round FA Cup match against Charlton Athletic on 14 February 1972. The greatest number of substitutes used in one season by Wolves under the single substitute rule was 35 in 1984–85, but after 1986–87 two substitutes were allowed and in seasons 1992–93 and 1993–94, 54 were used. Over the last few seasons, three substitutes have been allowed and 77 were used in 1996–97. The greatest number of substitute appearances for Wolves has been made by Robbie Dennison, who came on during 29 league games, with eight more in cup-ties. It was in 1987–88 that Joe Gallagher rewrote the Wolves records on the matter of substitutes with an extraordinary 13 league appearances in the substitute's shirt, a record which was equalled by Mixu Paatelainen in 1997–98.

**SUNDERLAND, ALAN** Alan Sunderland began his career with Wolverhampton Wanderers and turned professional in June 1971. During his seven seasons with the club he appeared in a number of different positions, having made his début in midfield in a 2–1 home win over Manchester City on 24 August 1971. By the end of his first season he had made eight league appearances including another four in the UEFA Cup, helping Wolves reach the final where they lost over two legs to Tottenham Hotspur. It was 1973–74 before he won a regular place on the Wolves side, scoring seven goals in 34 league games and appearing in the side that beat Manchester City in the final of the Football League Cup. During the club's relegation season of 1975–76 he was used as an emergency right-back but, when Wolves won the Second Division Championship the following season, he had reverted to the forward line and scored 16 goals in 41 games including a hat-trick in a 4–0 home win over Carlisle United. In November 1977, Sunderland, who had scored 35 goals in 198 games, joined Arsenal for £220,000. At the end of his first season

*Alan Sunderland*

with the Gunners he played in the FA Cup final against Ipswich and in 1978–79 scored six goals in the club's victorious FA Cup campaign. In 1979–80 he scored 28 first-team goals as Arsenal won the FA Cup and European Cup Winners' Cup, and won an England cap against Australia. A series of injuries then hampered his progress and, after scoring 92 goals in 281 first-team outings, he moved to Ipswich Town where he ended his league career.

**SUSPENSION** Whilst a number of Wolves players have served a suspension during their careers with the Molineux club, perhaps the one handed out to Billy Malpass, Tommy Dunn and Alf Griffin during the 1895–96 season is the strangest: the three players, who were all great servants of the club, were suspended for allegedly not trying on the pitch!

**SWINBOURNE, ROY** The son of a former Aston Villa reserve full-back, Roy Swinbourne joined the Wolves nursery side, Wath Wanderers, in 1944 before turning professional two years later. He made his league début for the Molineux club in a 1–1 draw at home to Fulham on 17 December 1949 and scored his first goal in a 3–2 defeat by Aston Villa on Boxing Day. He gained a regular place the following season when he topped the club's scoring charts with 22 goals in 48 League and Cup games including the first of seven hat-tricks for the club in a 7–1 home win over Bolton Wanderers. In 1951–52 a series of injuries forced him to miss more than half the club's games but in 1952–53 he was again Wolves' leading scorer with 21 goals. His total included hat-tricks against Manchester City (Home 7–3) and Manchester United (Home 6–2). He won a League Championship medal in 1953–54, his 24 goals in 40 league games including another hat-trick in a 4–1 home win over Blackpool. The following season, his fine goalscoring record led to his being capped for England 'B' against Germany. Swinbourne started the 1955–56 season in fine style, scoring 17 goals in the opening 12 matches, including four in the 7–2 home win over Manchester City and hat-tricks against Cardiff City (Away 9–1) and Huddersfield Town (Home 4–0). Sadly, Swinbourne injured a knee whilst trying to hurdle a group of cameramen sitting close to the touch-line behind the goal. Though at first it only seemed minor, it resulted in premature retirement for the likeable Swinbourne, who had scored 114 goals in 230 games.

# T

**TAYLOR, GERRY** Full-back Gerry Taylor made the first of 192 appearances for Wolves when he played in a goalless draw at home to Ipswich Town on New Year's Eve 1966. He went on to appear in 17 games that season as the club finished runners-up to Coventry City and won promotion to the First Division. However, over the next four seasons of top flight football, Taylor found himself in and out of the side and it wasn't until towards the end of the 1971–72 season that he established himself on the side. He played in both legs of the UEFA Cup final against Tottenham Hotspur and then appeared in 35 games in 1972–73 as Wolves finished fifth in Division One. After that he again found himself in and out of the side, being the reserve for the League Cup final against Manchester City at Wembley in 1974. Taylor left Molineux in 1976 to join the Staffordshire County Police force.

**TAYLOR, GRAHAM** After a playing career with Grimsby Town and Lincoln City, Graham Taylor began his managerial career with the Sincil Bank club and in 1976 took them to the Fourth Division title until, in June 1977, he received a good offer to take over the reins at Watford. There he stayed at Vicarage Road for over ten years, working alongside Elton John. He took Watford from the Fourth Division to runners-up spot in the First Division in 1982–83 and in 1984 he led them to their first ever FA Cup final, where they lost to Everton. Deciding he needed a fresh challenge, he became manager of Aston Villa in July 1987. At that stage, the club were in the Second Division and by the end of his first season in charge they were back in the top flight after finishing as runners-up to Millwall. After just avoiding relegation in 1988–89, they ended the following campaign as runners-up to Liverpool. Taylor left Villa Park in May 1990 to take over from Bobby Robson as England's team manager. However,

*Graham Taylor*

his career hit rock bottom with the European Championships of 1992 and within days of England failing to qualify for the 1994 World Cup finals, he had resigned. In April 1994 he was appointed manager of Wolverhampton Wanderers and in his first season led the Molineux club to fourth place in the First Division and the play-offs. Despite beating Bolton Wanderers 2–1 at home, however, Wolves lost 2–0 in the second leg. Expectations were high for the 1995–96 season, especially as money had been spent, but the performances on the pitch did not match up to the financial outlay and in December 1995 Graham Taylor was replaced by Mark McGhee. Taylor then returned to Vicarage Road as general manager and helped the Hornets win promotion to the Premier League via the play-offs.

**TAYLOR, JACK** Playing in the same Wolves side as his brother Frank, full-back Jack Taylor made his Wolves début in a 5–0 defeat at Brentford in February 1936, in the first side under the charge of Major Frank Buckley. In 1936–37, when Wolves finished fifth in Division One, Taylor appeared in 30 league games and all of the club's eight games in the FA Cup. He missed only three league games the following season as Wolves finished runners-up to League Champions Arsenal. During the 1938 close season, he was rather surprisingly allowed to leave Molineux after 89 appearances and join Norwich City. He made 50 appearances for the Canaries in peacetime football and 215 games in wartime soccer. At the end of the hostilities he joined Hull City and won a Third Division (North) Championship medal with them in 1948–49. After a short spell as player-manager of Weymouth, he managed both Queen's Park Rangers and Leeds United but without success.

**TELEVISION** In 1965, Wolverhampton Wanderers threatened the BBC with a court injunction claiming that the new drama series *United* was a thinly disguised version of their recent troubles!

**TENNANT, BILLY** Goalkeeper Billy Tennant joined Wolves from Hartshill United in January 1896 as a replacement for Billy Rose. His first game for the club was in a 2–1 defeat at Sheffield United, a month after his arrival at Molineux. Though he only appeared in 65 League and Cup games for Wolves, he was a member of the side that lost 2–1 to Sheffield Wednesday in the FA Cup final at the Crystal Palace at the end of his first season with the club. The Wolves keeper always wore a short-knotted neck-tie and had 100 per cent attendance in 1896–97 when Wolves finished tenth in the First Division. In a surprise move in 1898, he was sold to neighbours Walsall and played in 112 first-team games for the

Saddlers before being transferred to Grimsby Town in the summer of 1901. After just 13 games for the Mariners he was appointed the club's secretary-manager, although Grimsby's directors handled all playing matters.

**TEXACO CUP**  The predecessor of the Anglo-Scottish Cup, it was launched in 1970–71 and was for English, Irish and Scottish club sides not involved in European competition. In 1970–71, Wolves went all the way to the final, beating Dundee (Home 0–0, Away 2–1), Morton (Home 1–2, Away 3–0) and Derry City (Home 4–0, Away 1–0). In the final the Molineux club met Heart of Midlothian and, despite losing the second leg at Molineux to the only goal of the game, they had done enough to become the competition's first winners with a 3–1 triumph at Tynecastle, a game in which Hugh Curran scored two of the club's goals. Wolves next entered the competition in 1972–73 but after defeating Kilmarnock 5–1 on aggregate, went out 3–1 to Ipswich Town in the second round.

**THIRD DIVISION**  Wolves have had three spells in the Third Division, each one lasting just one season. Relegation to the Third Division was suffered at the end of George Jobey's first season as manager but in 1923–24 Wolves went straight back to Division Two as champions of the Third Division (North). The club were always in the leading pack and after a 20-match unbeaten run (24 November 1923 – 5 April 1924) they took the title one point ahead of Rochdale. Wolves' second spell in the Third Division was for season 1985–86 but this time the club finished 23rd and were relegated to the Fourth Division. This was undoubtedly the worst campaign in the club's history, as Wolves became only the second club to be relegated from the First Division to the Fourth Division in successive seasons. The team simply lacked confidence: they lost 25 of their 46 matches and suffered a number of heavy defeats. Wolves' last spell in the Third Division was in 1988–89 when they won the title once again with a club record total of 92 points. During the course of the season, they produced eight consecutive wins to equal the club record.

**THOMPSON, ANDY**  Determined little full-back Andy Thompson began his career with West Bromwich Albion but was never given a chance at The Hawthorns, and in November 1986 he joined

Wolverhampton Wanderers along with Steve Bull. Both players made their débuts for the Molineux club in a 3–0 home defeat by Wrexham. The following season he helped the club win the Fourth Division Championship and the Sherpa Van Trophy, appearing in 56 first-team games. He was the only ever-present in 1988–89, when Wolves won the Third Division title, and missed very few games over the next eight seasons. Awarded a testimonial by the club, his popularity was underlined by the fact that a crowd of almost 24,000 watched the game against Chelsea. Thompson went on to score 45 goals in 451 first-team games for Wolves before leaving Molineux in July 1997 to join Tranmere Rovers on a free transfer. At Prenton Park he missed just two games in his first season with the Birkenhead club and became Rovers' regular penalty-taker.

**THOMPSON, HARRY** Inside-forward Harry Thompson began his career with his home-town club Mansfield Town, though he failed to make the club's first team before leaving to join Wolves in March 1933. He had to wait until October 1935 before making his Football League début in a 3–1 defeat at Derby County. Despite that reversal he kept his place in the side for the next 11 matches and scored four goals including one in an 8–1 win over Blackpool. Though he never established himself as a first-team regular, he scored 17 goals in 73 games before leaving Wolves in December 1938 to join Sunderland for £7,500. During the war he 'guested' for York City before leaving Roker Park in 1946 to play for Northampton Town. He later held the post of player-manager at Headington United (now Oxford United) and in 1953–54 led the club to both the Southern League Championship and Cup, a season in which they also reached the fourth round of the FA Cup.

**THOMSON, BOBBY** Left-back Bobby Thomson was a polished defender whose performances in schoolboy football led to a number of Midlands clubs trying to sign him. Wolves won the chase and he made his début in a 2–1 FA Cup fourth-round defeat at home to West Bromwich Albion in front of 46,411 fans at Molineux. He soon established himself as a first-team regular and developed into an international player, gaining eight full caps for England before he was 22. He also appeared for the England Under-23s and the Football League, and he helped Wolves win promotion to the First Division in 1966–67. But in March 1969, after playing in 300 games for the Molineux club, he joined Birmingham City for £40,000. After making 68 league appearances for the Blues, where he also had a spell on loan with Walsall, he joined Luton Town before ending his league career with Port Vale. He then dropped into non-league football as player-manager of Stafford Rangers before leaving to run a sports shop in Sedgley.

**TONKS, JACK**  Speedy winger Jack Tonks played his early football with Walsall Unity before signing for Wolves in the summer of 1894. Though he failed to appear in any of the club's league games in 1894–95, he was drafted into the Molineux club's side for the FA Cup third-round tie at West Bromwich Albion, which the home side won 1–0. He made his league début at Preston North End in the second game of the 1895–96 season and scored one of Wolves' goals in a 4–3 defeat. That season he helped Wolves reach the FA Cup final where they lost 2–1 to Sheffield Wednesday at the Crystal Palace. He went on to score 23 goals in 119 games including the winner on his final appearance in a Wolves shirt at Sunderland on New Year's Day 1900. Tonks saw out his career with Walsall, where he made a further 20 league appearances.

**TOOTILL, ALF** Nicknamed 'The Birdcatcher', goalkeeper Alf Tootill began his playing career with Ramsbottom United in the Bury Amateur League before signing for Accrington Stanley in 1937. He had made 31 league appearances for the Peel Park club when Wolves paid £400 for his services in March 1929. He made his début in a 3–1 home win over Notts County (a match in which Frank Green scored a hat-trick), and then missed very few games over the next four seasons, being ever-present in 1931–32 when the club won the Second Division Championship. He had appeared in 143 first-team games for the Molineux club when he was transferred to Fulham in November 1932. The Lancashire-born keeper's last match for Wolves was against Arsenal at Molineux when he conceded seven goals! Tootill did well at Craven Cottage and made 214 appearances for Fulham before moving to Crystal Palace. He played regularly for the Selhurst Park club during the Second World War, appearing in 144 games before announcing his retirement in 1945.

**TRANSFERS**  The  record transfer fee received by the club was the £1.15 million that Manchester City paid for Steve Daley in

*Graham Turner*

September 1979. The record transfer fee paid out by Wolves was £1.85 million to Bradford City for Dean Richards in May 1995.

**TURNER, GRAHAM** A former England Youth international, Graham

Turner appeared in 634 league games for Wrexham, Chester and Shrewsbury between 1965 and 1984. He was appointed player-manager of Shrewsbury Town in 1978 and in 1978–79 led them to the Third Division Championship. They also reached the sixth round of the FA Cup that season before losing at Highbury in a replay. In July 1984 he accepted a lucrative offer to take over at Villa Park. However, after two mediocre seasons and a poor start to the 1986–87 campaign, he was sacked. A month later he was offered the manager's job at Wolverhampton Wanderers. The Molineux club were near the foot of the Fourth Division and heavily in debt. After a disappointing start which saw Wolves knocked out of the FA Cup by non-league Chorley, Turner made some important signings, including future England international Steve Bull, and took the club to the Fourth Division play-offs where they lost, surprisingly, to Aldershot. However, the following season they won the Fourth Division Championship and the Sherpa Van Trophy. In 1988–89 they won the Third Division title in style but struggled in the Second Division. After a poor start to the 1991–92 season, there was talk that Turner would be sacked, but results improved and he stayed until March 1994 when he was replaced by Graham Taylor.

# U

**UEFA CUP** Entering the UEFA Cup for the first time in 1971–72, Wolves came very close to becoming the first Midlands team to win a major European competition. In the first round, they strolled past Academica Coimbra 7–1 on aggregate with Derek Dougan scoring a second-leg hat-trick at Molineux. In round two, Wolves faced Dutch opposition in Den Haag and again won 7–1 on aggregate. The second leg of this tie was memorable simply because the Dutch side managed to score three goals yet still be on the losing side of 4–0, as each effort was in their own net! In the third round Wolves beat Carl Zeiss Jena, winning by a single goal in Germany, before a comparatively simple home victory of 3–0 in which Dougan scored two of the goals. The club's first real test came in the quarter-finals against Juventus. After the Italians had taken an early lead in front of a 35,000-strong volatile home crowd, Jim McCalliog snatched a vital equaliser midway through the second half. In the return leg at Molineux, the Italians rested a number of star players, preferring to save them for a Serie A decider against Torino the following Sunday. This gave Wolves an advantage and goals from Hegan and Dougan took the Molineux club into the semi-final where they faced Ferencvaros of Hungary. The first leg took place in the Nep Stadium on Hungary's National Liberation Day. After John Richards had given Wolves an early lead, the Hungarian side scored two goals in the space of three minutes just after the half-hour mark. Bernard Shaw, who handled in the area for Ferencvaros' first goal, did the same again, but this time Phil Parkes saved Szoke's effort. A few minutes later, Frank Munro forced home David Wagstaffe's corner and Wolves went into the return leg at Molineux all-square at 2–2. Steve Daley, who was making his European début, scored after just 25 seconds before Munro headed home to make it 2–0 on the night and 4–2 on aggregate. Two minutes into the second-half,

Ku pulled a goal back for the Hungarians who were then awarded their third penalty of the tie after Sunderland had handled in the box. Parkes again saved with his trailing leg as Szoke aimed the ball into the centre of the goal and Wolves were through to the first ever all-English final in a European competition, against Tottenham Hotspur. Spurs won the first leg at Molineux, 2–1, with Martin Chivers scoring both their goals and Jim McCalliog netting for Wolves. In the second leg at White Hart Lane, Spurs extended their lead when Alan Mullery somehow headed in Martin Peters' cross. Just before half-time, David Wagstaffe scored from fully 30 yards. Though Dougan headed home he was given offside; Wolves could not break down the stubborn Spurs defence and lost 3–2 on aggregate. In 1973–74 Wolves knocked out Portuguese side Belenenses 4–1 on aggregate but then lost on the away goals rule to Lokomotiv Leipzig after winning the second leg at Molineux 4–1 following a 3–0 defeat in East Germany. The following season, Wolves went out at the first hurdle to FC Porto. After losing the first leg in Portugal 4–1, Wolves won the return 3–1 but an own goal by Geoff Palmer put paid to their chances of completing a remarkable fightback. The club last participated in the UEFA Cup in 1980–81 but again went out of the competition in the first round, losing 3–2 on aggregate to PSV Eindhoven.

**UNDEFEATED** Wolves have remained undefeated at home throughout just one league season. That was in 1923–24 when they won 18 and drew 3 of their games at Molineux when winning the Third Division (North) Championship. The club's best and longest undefeated home sequence in the Football League is of 27 matches between 24 March 1923 and 6 September 1924. Wolves' longest run of undefeated Football League matches home and away is 20 between 24 November 1923 and 5 April 1924.

**UTILITY PLAYERS** A utility player is one of those particularly gifted footballers who can play in several different positions. Three of Wolves' earliest utility players were Jack Brodie, John Baynton and Albert Groves. English international Jack Brodie played in virtually every position during the club's pre-league days and in the first few seasons of league football. John Baynton played for Wolves for 12 years and, in that time, appeared in eight different positions for the club including goalkeeper. Groves played in all the half-back positions, and at inside-forward and centre-forward, scoring ten goals during the club's 1912–13 season. Tom Galley was a great servant of Wolverhampton Wanderers and would play in whatever position he was asked. He too appeared in all the half-back positions, and at inside-forward and centre-forward, and captained Wolves to the 1942 Wartime League (North) Cup final. Gus McLean also appeared in all the half-back positions and at centre-forward, but it was in both full-back positions that he excelled. After the mid-1960s, players were encouraged to become more adaptable and to see their roles as less stereotypical. At the same time, much less attention was paid to the implication of wearing a certain numbered shirt. Accordingly, some of the more versatile players came to wear all the different numbered shirts at some stage or another, although this did not necessarily indicate an enormous variety of positions.

# V

**VAUGHAN, NIGEL** Nigel Vaughan began his Football League career with Newport County and went on to score 32 goals in 224 league appearances for the Somerton Park club. At Newport, he won the first of 10 Welsh caps when he played against Yugoslavia. He joined Cardiff City in September 1983 as part of the unusual five-man exchange deal between the two clubs. In 1984–85 he was City's top scorer with 16 league goals but, despite his efforts, the club were relegated to the Third Division. He was the club's top scorer again the following season, but the Bluebirds were relegated for a second successive season and dropped into the league's basement. In 1986–87 he became dissatisfied with Fourth Division football and after scoring 54 goals in 178 games, left to join Wolverhampton Wanderers for a fee of £12,000. He made his début for the Molineux club at Ninian Park where he came on as a substitute and scored in a 3–2 defeat. He won successive League Championship medals as Wolves won the Third and Fourth Division titles, and was a member of the side that beat Burnley in the Sherpa Van Trophy final at Wembley. He had scored 13 goals in 118 games when he was transferred to Hereford United, later ending his career playing non-league football for both Worcester City and Newport AFC.

**VENUS, MARK** Versatile defender Mark Venus began his Football League career with his home-town club Hartlepool United before joining Leicester City on a free transfer in September 1985. He had appeared in 69 first-team games for the Foxes when Wolves paid £40,000 for his services in March 1988. He made his début in a 1–0 home defeat by Peterborough United but in only his fourth appearance he suffered a bad injury and had to miss the rest of the season. However he played in 35 games the following season when

Wolves won the Third Division Championship, finishing eight points ahead of runners-up Sheffield United. Able to play in a variety of positions, he remained a first-team regular with the Molineux club until the summer of 1997 when, after making 338 appearances, he joined Ipswich Town as part of the deal that saw Steve Sedgley move in the opposite direction.

**VICTORIAN INDUCEMENT** The concept of illegally transferred players is not new in the game. In the 1890–91 season, Wolverhampton Wanderers induced Preston North End player Sam Thomson to join them without the Lancashire club's permission and they were fined £50 for their misconduct!

**VICTORIES IN A SEASON – HIGHEST** In seasons 1957–58 and 1958–59, Wolves won 28 of their 42 league fixtures and took the First Division Championship in both seasons.

**VICTORIES IN A SEASON – LOWEST** Wolves' poorest performance was in 1983–84 when they won only six matches out of their 42 league games and finished bottom of the First Division.

**VIZARD, TED** Ted Vizard played rugby for Penarth and football for Barry Town before being recommended to Bolton Wanderers by an old school friend. The Lancashire club signed him and in November 1910 he made his début in a 3–0 win over Gainsborough Trinity. The first of his 22 Welsh caps came in 1911, only two months after his first appearance in the league, and his last in October 1926 when he was 37. During the First World War, Vizard served in the RAF and 'guested' for Chelsea, alongside another Bolton player, Joe Smith. The pair formed an ideal partnership and helped the Stamford Bridge club win the 1918 London v Lancashire Cup final. Ted Vizard was a member of Bolton's successful FA Cup-winning teams of 1923 and 1926 and, though not a prolific scorer, netted a hat-trick in a 3–0 defeat of Arsenal in October 1925. He made the last of his 512 appearances, in which he had scored 70 goals, in March 1931. At the age of 41, he was the oldest player to appear in a first-team game for the club until Peter Shilton kept goal for the Trotters in 1995. After leaving Bolton he became manager of Swindon Town and later took charge of Queen's Park Rangers before being appointed manager of Wolverhampton Wanderers in

April 1944 as a replacement for Major Buckley. Vizard, who got the job from almost 100 applicants, laid the foundations for future success at the Molineux club. Unfortunately, he was not the game's greatest motivator and in the summer of 1948 he was replaced by his assistant Stan Cullis, despite taking the club to third place in the First Division in 1946–47.

# W

**WAGSTAFFE, DAVID** David Wagstaffe began his league career with his home-town club Manchester City and, in six seasons at Maine Road, scored 8 goals in 161 games before leaving to join Wolverhampton Wanderers for a fee of £30,000 in December 1964. He made his début for the Molineux club in a 1–0 home defeat by Aston Villa on Boxing Day and, though they were relegated at the end of that season, Wagstaffe had already endeared himself to the Wolves faithful. When Wolves won promotion to the First Division in 1966-67, Wagstaffe was the club's only ever-present. He helped Wolves reach the UEFA Cup final in 1972 and win the Football League Cup in 1974. Possessing a terrific shot and the most accurate of crosses, Wagstaffe stayed at Molineux for 11 seasons, scoring 31 goals in 404 first-team appearances before joining Blackburn Rovers in 1976. As a Blackburn player, he had the unenviable distinction of being the first Football League player to be shown a red card when being sent off! He later had a spell with Blackpool before returning to Ewood Park and retiring in May 1979 after appearing in 564 league games for his four clubs.

**WALKER, GEORGE** Wednesfield-born defender George Walker joined Wolves from Willenhall Pickwick in the summer of 1899, primarily as cover for Ted 'Cock' Pheasant. After playing the entire 1899–1900 season in the club's reserves, he was given his first-team début against Bolton Wanderers in September 1900 in a match that ended all square at 1–1. After that, Walker, who was a fine utility defender, gave the Molineux club five seasons' excellent service. When he did deputise for Pheasant, he formed an outstanding partnership at the heart of the Wolves defence with Jack White-house, and went on to play in 132 games before leaving to join Crystal Palace, who were then a Southern League club. He was the

*David Wagstaffe*

father of England international, Billy Walker, and the brother of George, who played for Aston Villa.

**WALKER, JOHNNY**  Glasgow-born Johnny Walker joined Wolves in July 1947 as an inside-forward or wing-half but had to wait until 18 February 1950 before making his début in a 1–0 home win over Portsmouth. The following Saturday he scored twice in a 4–1 defeat of Derby County and ended the season with 8 goals in 12 games. In 1950–51 he netted 11 league goals in 20 games and five more in the club's run to the FA Cup semi-finals. After suffering from a series of niggling injuries, Walker found it difficult to regain his first-team place and, having scored 26 goals in just 44 games, he left Molineux to join Southampton. The Saints, who paid £12,000 for his services, must have been well satisfied with the transaction, for in five years at The Dell he scored 48 goals in 172 games. In December 1957 he joined Reading and, after being moved into a far more deep-lying position, he netted 24 goals in 287 league appearances for the then Elm Park club.

**WARTIME FOOTBALL**  In spite of the outbreak of the First World War in 1914, the major Football Leagues embarked upon their planned programme of matches for the ensuing season and these were completed on schedule at the end of April the following year when Wolves finished fourth in Division Two. Though a Wartime League Emergency competition was introduced in 1915, the Molineux club decided not to enter. In complete contrast to the events of 1914, once war was declared on 3 September 1939, the Football League programme of 1939–40 was suspended and for a while there was no football of any description. The game continued later on a regional basis and Wolves initially played in the Midland Regional League, which they won. The Wolves board decided against playing any football in 1940–41 but the following season joined the Football League (South). That season Wolves beat Sunderland in a two-legged League Cup final, 6–3 on aggregate. Over the next few seasons, Wolves played in the Football League (North) and in 1944–45 reached the semi-final of the League (North) Cup only to lose to Bolton Wanderers. During the hostilities, Molineux was used as the headquarters for Air Raid Precautions, and the club records were moved out for safe keeping.

**WATNEY CUP** This was Britian's first commercially sponsored tournament and was a pre-season competition for the top two highest-scoring teams in each division of the Football League the previous season. Clubs could only compete if they had no other European involvement. In the club's only match in the competition on 29 July 1972, Wolves travelled to Bristol Rovers for a first-round match but lost 2–0.

**WATSON, TED** Full-back Ted Watson joined Wolves from Pontypridd FC in May 1921 and made his début in a 1–0 win at Leicester City on 29 October 1921. Over the next couple of seasons, Watson appeared in only 17 games but by the start of the 1923–24 season, he had established himself as the club's first-choice right-back. During that campaign, in which Wolves won the Third Division (North) Championship, Watson missed just one game, a 2–1 defeat at Walsall – one of only three reversals the club suffered that season. Watson appeared in 206 League and Cup games for Wolves before being transferred to Coventry City in March 1929. He made 92 appearances for the Sky Blues before leaving to play non-league football with Oakengates Town.

**WEATHER CONDITIONS** On Saturday, 1 September 1906, Wolves played their first ever Second Division game against Hull City at Molineux. Full-back Jack Jones scored for Wolves in a 1–1 draw on what is thought to be the hottest day on which the league programme has ever been completed – the temperature was over 90°F (32°C).

**WEAVER, REG** A former winner of the Welsh Powderhall sprint at Caerphilly, Reg Weaver was one of the fastest forwards in the game and, after beginning his league career with Newport County, joined Wolves in November 1927. After making his début in a 2–2 home draw against Notts County, he went on to score 11 goals in 22 games, ten of them coming in six consecutive games when he scored a hat-trick in a 5–2 win over Bristol City. That season he appeared on the same Wolves side as his brother Walter on five occasions. In 1928–29 he was the club's top scorer with 18 goals in 28 games, including netting his second hat-trick in a 5–0 win at Millwall. Weaver had scored 29 goals in 50 games when he left Molineux in March 1929 to play for Chelsea. Unable to win a regular place in the London club's side, he moved to Bradford City but left after nine months to have a brief spell with Chesterfield before returning to Newport County where he ended his career.

**WESTCOTT, DENNIS** One of the greatest ever goalscorers to wear the old gold and black strip of Wolverhampton Wanderers, Dennis Westcott joined New Brighton during the 1932–33 season before switching to Molineux in February 1937. In that time, he had won Schoolboy International honours and had an unsuccessful trial with West Ham United. He made his début for Wolves in an FA Cup fifth-round tie against Grimsby Town, scoring one of the goals in a 6–2 win. His league début followed three days later at Manchester City and in only his fourth league appearance he scored both goals in a 2–1 win over Stoke City. In 1937–38 he was the club's leading scorer with 22 goals in 28 games including 4 goals against Leicester City in a 10–1 win for the Molineux club and a hat-trick against Swansea Town in a 4–0 FA Cup win. In 1938–39, Westcott netted a remarkable 43 goals in 43 league and cup appearances and won an FA Cup final runners-up medal after Wolves had been beaten 4–1 by Portsmouth in the Wembley final. He netted three hat-tricks in the league against Chelsea (Home 3–1), Grimsby Town (Home 5–0) and Brentford (Home 5–2), and then scored another four goals against Grimsby in the FA Cup semi-final at Old Trafford, as the Mariners were again beaten 5–0. During the hostilities, Westcott scored 91 goals in 76 games including ten hat-tricks, five of which came in the 1939–40 season. He played in the Wartime League Cup match against Sunderland in 1942 and scored three of Wolves' goals in their 6–3 aggregate win over the Wearsiders. He was very unlucky not to win full international honours for England, though he did play in four Victory Internationals and represented the Football League. In 1946–47 he established another club record (which still stands today) of 38 league goals in a season, a total which included Westcott scoring four goals in successive games against Liverpool (Away 5–1) and Bolton Wanderers (Home 5–0). He scored 124 goals in 144 League and Cup games – a total of 215 goals in 220 games if you include the war years before he left Molineux to join Blackburn Rovers. After scoring 37 goals in 63 league games for the Ewood Park club, he signed for Manchester City where he netted 37 goals in 72 games before ending his career with Chesterfield. After that he had a short spell playing non-league football with Stafford Rangers until he died suddenly at the age of 43 in 1960.

**WHARTON, TERRY** Bolton-born Terry Wharton followed his father in becoming an old-style winger in the Football League. His father had played in more than 250 league games for Plymouth, Preston, Manchester City, Blackburn and Newport. Terry Wharton scored on his début for Wolves in a 2–0 home win over Ipswich Town on 11 November 1961, having signed professional forms some two years earlier. The club's first-choice right-winger for the next five and a half seasons, he netted his first hat-trick for the club in March 1963 as West Bromwich Albion were beaten 7–0. He was in the Wolves' side that lost their First Division status in 1964–65 but two seasons later he helped the Molineux club win promotion to the First Division, netting another hat-trick in a 7–1 home win over Cardiff City. He had scored 79 goals in 242 games for Wolves when he joined his home-town club, Bolton Wanderers, for £70,000, the Lancashire club's record buy at the time. Wharton replaced Francis Lee, who had just been sold to Manchester City, and became Bolton's penalty-taker. Sadly, injuries did not allow him to perform consistently, though in 1969–70 he missed only four games. Early the following term he hit his first hat-trick for the club in a 4–2 win over Luton Town. After failing to live up to his early promise at Bolton, where he scored 30 goals in 110 games, he left and joined Crystal Palace. He made 20 league appearances for Palace and in December 1973 played his last game in the Football League. It was his only game for Walsall.

**WHITEHOUSE, JACK** Jack Whitehouse joined Wolves from Wednesbury Town in the summer of 1900 and spent his first season with the club playing in the reserves. He made his first-team début in the opening game of the 1901–02 season, partnering Ted Pheasant in the heart of the defence as Wolves beat Nottingham Forest 2–0. Over the next five seasons, Whitehouse was a first-team regular, though he was sent off once and the resultant suspension caused him to miss a number of matches. His only goal for the club came in the FA Cup tie at Derby County at the Baseball Ground in February 1904 when his long-range shot earned Wolves a replay. Whitehouse had appeared in 155 first-team games when in the summer of 1906 he left the club following an argument with team-mates and other members of staff. He joined Stourbridge before later playing for a number of local clubs – Bloxwich Strollers, Darlaston, Dudley and Gornal Wood.

**WILLIAMS, BERT** One of the greatest names in the history of Wolverhampton Wanderers, goalkeeper Bert Williams began his professional career with Walsall and made 28 league and Southern Section Cup appearances before the outbreak of the Second World War. During the hostilities he served with the RAF but in September 1945 he joined Wolves for a bargain price of £3,500. He made his league début for the Molineux club in a 6–1 home win over Arsenal on the opening day of the 1946–47 season. Over the next 11 seasons, Williams was the club's first-choice keeper, his outstanding displays winning him 24 caps for England. The first of these came three weeks after he had won an FA Cup winners' medal against Leicester City, when he played in a 3–1 win over France in Paris. Williams won a League Championship medal in 1953–54 and went on to play in 419 League and Cup games for Wolves before retiring at the end of the 1956–57 season and handing over to Malcolm Finlayson. He later ran a successful sports outfitter's shop in Bilston and a goalkeeping school before working in an engineering firm.

**WILSHAW, DENNIS** After some prolific goalscoring feats in the North Staffordshire League, Dennis Wilshaw signed for Wolves as a professional in 1944, but was allowed to join Walsall on loan. He did so well with the Saddlers, scoring 21 goals in 87 games, that he was recalled to Molineux in September 1948. On his league début on 12 March 1949, Wilshaw blasted a hat-trick in a 3–0 home win over Newcastle United and ended the season with 10 goals in 11 league games. He was, nevertheless, still classed as a reserve to players like Jesse Pye and Roy Swinbourne and over the next three seasons appeared in just 37 games, scoring 13 goals. He finally established himself as a first-team regular for the Molineux club in 1952–53 when he scored 18 goals in 30 games and then in 1953–54 when the club won the League Championship for the first time in their history – Wilshaw was top scorer with 25 goals, his total including a hat-trick in an 8–1 win over Chelsea. Wilshaw won 12 full caps for England, making his first appearance against Wales at Ninian Park when he scored twice in a 4–1 win. The following year he played in the World Cup finals and in 1955, on his first appearance at Wembley, he scored four goals in England's 7–2 win over Scotland. He stayed at Molineux, where he had scored 117 goals in 232 games, until December 1957 when he was transferred to his home-town club, Stoke City. Wilshaw spent four years at the Victoria Ground and had scored 50 goals in 108 League and Cup games when a broken leg in a match at Newcastle United forced him into retirement.

**WILSON, LES**  Les Wilson joined Wolves as a junior in 1963 before turning professional in September 1964 and making his début in a 3–1 defeat at Middlesbrough on 18 December 1965. It was his only appearance that season and, in fact, the first of just 22 over the next three campaigns before he established himself as a first-team regular in 1968–69. Able to play in midfield or defence, he appeared in 116 games for Wolves before leaving to join Bristol City in November 1971. He had a brief loan spell with the Ashton Gate club in March of that year, featuring prominently in the club's escape from relegation. He had made 45 appearances for City when, following a brief top-flight return with Norwich City in September 1973, he moved to Vancouver Whitecaps and became coach. Now based in British Columbia, he is the National Team's Administrator of the Canadian Football Association.

**WOOD, HARRY**  Harry Wood began his career with his home-town club, Walsall Swifts, before joining Wolverhampton Wanderers in 1887. He scored on his début in a 7–0 FA Cup win over Derby St Luke's and had netted 46 goals in 87 first-team outings when in the summer of 1891 he returned to play for Walsall Swifts. Wood, who by that time had been capped twice by England, soon returned to Wolves and, in April 1892, netted a hat-trick in a 6–3 win at Aston Villa. That season Wood was top scorer with 16 goals, a feat he achieved twice in the following three seasons. He had won an FA Cup winners' medal in 1893 but, towards the end of his second spell with the club, he was moved into defence and this led to his becoming unsettled at Molineux after scoring 126 goals in 289 games. In 1898 Southampton's trainer, Dawson, was visiting relatives in the Birmingham area and, on hearing of Wood's plight, decided to investigate the matter further. After making inquiries in a local pub, he contacted Wood who signed there and then for the Saints. Nicknamed 'The Wolf', he scored 16 goals in his first season with the club, including a hat-trick in the 6–0 home win over Sheppey United as Southampton won the Southern League Championship. He was soon made captain and led the club through one of the most successful periods in the Saints' history. They reached the FA Cup final in 1900 and 1902 and won the Southern League Championship in seasons 1900–01, 1902–03 and 1903–04. In 1905, after scoring 62 goals in 158 games for Southampton, he hung up his boots to become Portsmouth's trainer, a position he held for five years.

**WOODFIELD, DAVE** Leamington Spa-born centre-half Dave Woodfield joined Wolves as an amateur in January 1959 before turning professional in October of the following year. After some impressive performances for the club's Central League side, he broke into the first team towards the end of the 1961–62 season and made his début in a 1–1 home draw against Chelsea. After starting the 1962–63 season as the club's first-choice centre-half, he held his place for the next eight seasons, appearing in 276 League and Cup games, scoring 15 goals. Five of those goals came in a four-match spell towards the end of the 1965–66 season when he was asked to line-up as a makeshift centre-forward. Forming a fine central defensive partnership with John Holsgrove, he helped Wolves win promotion to the First Division in 1966–67. In the top flight, Woodfield appeared in 38 games, his only goal being the winner against Fulham on 16 December 1967. He finally left Molineux in September 1971 and joined Watford, where he made 15 league appearances before leaving the first-class game.

**WOODRUFF, BOBBY** A member of Swindon Town's successful young side which gained promotion to the Second Division in 1962–63, Bobby Woodruff made 180 league appearances for the County Ground club before being transferred to Wolverhampton Wanderers for £40,000 in March 1964. He played his first game for the club in a 5–1 home win over Birmingham City and in 1964–65 was Wolves' second highest scorer with 11 goals in 33 games, including a hat-trick in a 3–0 home win over Sunderland. Known for his long-throw 'specials', Woodruff left Molineux in the summer of 1966 after scoring 21 goals in 72 games and joined Crystal Palace for £35,000. He helped Palace win promotion to the First Division in 1968–69, but only played a few games in the top flight before leaving to sign for Cardiff City. Over the next five seasons, Woodruff proved himself to be the Bluebirds' most reliable and versatile player, once scoring six goals in six games when asked to play centre-forward. He later ended his league career with Newport County where he took

*Bobby Woodruff*

his total of Football League appearances for his five clubs to 566 before finishing his career in Welsh League soccer.

**WOOLDRIDGE, BILLY** Though he could occupy any outfield position, it was as a goalscoring centre-forward that Billy Wooldridge made his name with Wolves. He joined the Molineux club from Cradley St Luke's in the summer of 1899 and made his début in a 1–1 home draw against Sheffield Wednesday on Boxing Day 1900. He was the club's leading goalscorer for the next three seasons, with a best of 19 goals in 34 games in 1903–04. After sharing the position with Jack Smith in 1904–05, he topped the goalscoring charts again the following season when he netted a hat-trick in the final game of the campaign as Wolves beat Derby County 7–0. Wooldridge had scored his first hat-trick for the club in a 5–1 FA Cup win over New Brighton in his first season in the side. At this time he also scored four goals for England in an unofficial international against Germany (a 10–1 win) and scored a hat-trick for the Football League against the Irish League. For the 1906–07 season, Wooldridge was moved to centre-half and captained the side to success in the 1908 FA Cup final over Newcastle United. He went on to score 89 goals in 356 League and Cup games before hanging up his boots at the end of the 1910–11 season.

**WORST STARTS** The club's worst-ever start to a season was in 1983–84. It took 15 league games to record the first victory of the season, drawing four and losing ten of the opening fixtures. The run ended with a 3–1 success over West Bromwich Albion at The Hawthorns on 26 November 1983, with Danny Cranie scoring two of the goals.

**WREKIN CUP** The Wrekin Cup was the first trophy won by the club. Wolves won through to the final of the 1883–84 competition by beating St Paul's (Lozells) 7–0 and Stafford Road 4–2. In the final, they beat Hadley 11–0 with Jack Brodie scoring five of the goals and Arthur Lowder netting a hat-trick.

**WRIGGLESWORTH, BILLY** After playing non-league football for Frickley Colliery, outside-left Billy Wrigglesworth joined Chesterfield where his form for the Saltergate club led to a number of clubs showing an interest in him. He joined Wolves just after the start of the 1934–35 season and scored 7 goals in 22 outings in his first term with the club. He went on to score 22 goals in 58 League and Cup games but, after losing his first-team place to George Ashall, he left Molineux to join Manchester United. At Old Trafford, Wrigglesworth was a great success, scoring 37 goals in 114 appearances for the club. Included in this total were 27 goals in 77 wartime outings – Wrigglesworth scoring five goals on 25 November 1939 as Port Vale were beaten 8–1. He signed for Bolton Wanderers in January 1947 but after just 13 games for the Trotters he joined Southampton before ending his career with Reading.

**WRIGHT, BILLY** Born in Ironbridge, Shropshire, Billy Wright was the model professional. In 117 wartime outings, 654 league and cup games and 105 internationals, he was never sent off or cautioned. A mark of the esteem in which he was held was shown by his election as an honorary life-member of the Football Association. A centre-forward as a schoolboy, once scoring ten goals in a match, he was rejected by Major Frank Buckley as being too small. Thankfully, Buckley changed his mind and signed him on amateur forms in 1939. He made his début for a Wolves senior XI against Notts County in February 1941 but, after turning professional, he broke his ankle in a cup-tie against West Bromwich Albion and it was thought at the time that he would never play football again. However, he was soon back in training and when the war ended he made his Football League début on the opening day of the 1946–47 season against Arsenal at Molineux when Wolves won 6–1. He played at left-half alongside Stan Cullis, from whom he took over as captain the next season, leading Wolves to FA Cup success in 1949 and to the League Championship in 1953–54, 1957–58 and 1958–59. It was inevitable that his consistent displays at wing-half would lead to his selection for the England side and, after appearing in seven wartime internationals, his first full appearance was in a 7–2 win over Ireland in Belfast in September 1946. Wright regarded playing for his country as the highest honour his chosen profession could give him. He captained England on 90 occasions. If one match more than any other can be described as the climax of his career, then it has to be England against Scotland at Wembley on 11 April 1959 – the match gave him his 100th cap and made him the first man in the history of football to pass this milestone. The previous year, just after the World Cup in Sweden, Wright had married Joy

*Billy Wright*

Beverley of the internationally known Beverley Sisters. At the end of the 1958–59 season, Wright decided to retire as a player while he was still at the top. He was 35 and though he could have held his own for another season or two, he knew in his heart that the pace was beginning to tell. Although at 5ft 8ins he was on the small side for a centre-half, he was rarely, if ever, beaten in the air. A fine reader of the game, he tackled firmly and would distribute the ball intelligently. As a captain he led from the front, inspiring those around him and setting a wonderful example to his team-mates. Wright was awarded the CBE for his services to football, and he became team manager of England's Under-23 and Youth sides, an FA Staff Coach, a TV personality and disc jockey, a regular contributor to newspapers and magazines and a players' agent. He became a Wolves director in 1990 and a new £5 million stand at Molineux has been named after him. Sadly, Billy Wright, the greatest player in Wolves' history, died at his home in Barnet on 3 September 1994, aged 70.

**WYKES, DAVID** Walsall-born David Wykes, who went on to appear in every forward position for Wolves, played his early football with Bloxwich Strollers and Wednesbury Town before joining his home-town club. Wolves signed him from Walsall in the summer of 1888 and he made his league début in a 4–0 home defeat by champions Preston North End. His best season for the club in terms of goals scored was 1889–90 when he netted 15 goals in 22 league games including a hat-trick in a 5–1 home win over Bolton Wanderers. Wykes went on to score 69 goals in 178 games but, just 24 hours after making the last of those appearances in a 1–0 home win over Stoke in October 1895, he died of typhoid fever and pneumonia in a Walsall hospital.

# X

**'X'** In football 'x' traditionally stands for a draw. The club record for the number of draws in a season was in 1990–91 when they drew 19 of their matches.

**XMAS DAY** There was a time when Football League matches were regularly played on Christmas Day, but in recent years the game's authorities have dropped the fixture from their calendar. The last time Wolverhampton Wanderers played on Christmas Day was in 1956 when they went down 2–1 at Charlton Athletic. The first occasion Wolves played a league game on Christmas Day was 1901 when they lost 3–1 at Derby County. The club's first win on Christmas Day came in 1907 when Billy Harrison scored the only goal of the game against Gainsborough Trinity. On Christmas Day 1926, Tom Phillipson scored five of Wolves' goals in a 7–2 home win over Bradford City. Another scorer of a hat-trick on Christmas Day was Charlie Phillips who netted three in a 5–1 defeat of Derby County in 1934. It hasn't always been plain sailing for Wolves on Christmas Day, however: in 1914 they lost 5–1 at Hull City; in 1922 they were beaten 7–1 at Coventry City; and in 1933, Aston Villa gained revenge for a 3–1 defeat on Christmas Day the previous year when they beat Wolves 6–2.

# Y

**YOUNG, BOB** Much travelled centre-half Bob Young played for St Mirren before moving south of the border to play for West Ham United. After just one season at Upton Park he was on the move again, this time to Middlesbrough. He had two seasons at Ayresome Park before joining Everton in October 1910. Wolves signed Young from the Goodison Park club in October 1911 for a fee of £200, and the tough-tackling Scottish defender made his début in a 1–1 home draw against Bradford. He liked nothing better than to support the attack and, in 73 games, scored 11 goals – one of them with his head from fully 20 yards. Sadly, injury and illness forced his retirement from the game in May 1914.

**YOUNGEST PLAYER** The youngest player to appear in a first-class fixture for Wolverhampton Wanderers is Jimmy Mullen, who played in the First Division match against Leeds United (Home 4–1) on 18 February 1939 when he was 16 years 43 days old. During the Second World War, Cameron Buchanan was just 14 years 57 days old when he played against West Bromwich Albion (Home 2–0) on 26 September 1942.

**YOUTH CUP** Wolverhampton Wanderers have won the FA Youth Cup on just one occasion but have been beaten finalists on four occasions. The club won the trophy in 1957–58 when they beat Chelsea 7–6 on aggregate after losing the first leg at Stamford Bridge 5–1. In the second leg at Molineux, Ted Farmer scored four first-half goals to level the scores. In the second-half Cliff Durandt scored two goals to put Wolves 6–0 up on the night before a certain Jimmy Greaves pulled one back for the London side. Wolves were finalists on four other occasions with the following results:

1952–53    v Manchester United (Home 2–2 Away 1–7)
                Lost 3–9 on aggregate
1953–54    v Manchester United (Home 4–4 Away 0–1)
                Lost 4–5 on aggregate
1961–62    v Newcastle United (Home 1–1 Away 0–1)
                Lost 1–2 on aggregate
1975–76    v West Bromwich Albion (Home 0–2 Away 0–3)
                Lost 0–5 on aggregate

The club have also been beaten semi-finalists on three occasions, losing 4–2 to West Ham United in 1962–63; 3–0 on aggregate to Arsenal in 1970–71; and 7–2 on aggregate to Watford in 1981–82.

# Z

**ZENITH** Few fans will argue over which has been the greatest moment in the history of the club. In the space of six years in the 1950s, Wolves won the League Championship three times in seasons 1953–54, 1957–58 and 1958–59. It was around this time that Wolves beat Moscow Spartak and Honved, prompting manager Stan Cullis to boast that his team were champions of the world!

**ZENITH DATA SYSTEMS CUP** The Zenith Data Systems Cup replaced the Simod Cup for the 1989–90 season. Wolves' first match in the competition saw them lose 1–0 at Sheffield United and, though they beat Leicester City 1–0 at Filbert Street in the first round of the 1990–91 competition, they bowed out at the next hurdle, losing 2–1 at home to Leeds United. The club's last game in the competition came on 1 October 1991 when they travelled to Grimsby Town and lost 1–0 in front of a Blundell Park crowd of just 1,593.